PROJECT ALIEN MIND CONTROL -- UFO REVIEW SPECIAL

IS THERE AN ALIEN MIND CONTROL PROGRAM?

Mankind is being enslaved by non-human forces who are technologically, psychically, and dimensionally superior to us (but not necessarily spiritually, and therein lies our freedom).

They consist of multiple factions, spanning multiple dimensions and locations in space/time, all here to take a slice of the human pie. Their ultimate goal is to assimilate us into their fascist empire and parasitically exploit us for our biological, etheric, and physical resources.

Through covert manipulation and hyper-dimensional tricks that employ time travel, they have secretly manipulated and exploited humanity in every way conceivable since the birth of our race, and even our origins are suspect and bear the signs of genetic engineering.

We are now seeing their plans overtly manifest with the abduction and hybrid breeding program, and their imminent portrayal as saviors to a human race gone mad with world conflict. If the world accepts them as saviors, individual freedom as we know it will become snuffed like a blown candle, leaving only darkness.

COURTESY OF MONTALK.NET

PROJECT ALIEN MIND CONTROL -- UFO REVIEW SPECIAL

ULTRA-TERRESTRIALS ARE HERE SCREWING WITH OUR MINDS
By Timothy Green Beckley

DO ALIEN VISITORS FROM OTHER WORLDS WALK AMONG US?

PROJECT ALIEN MIND CONTROL

CONTENTS

Spreading The Truth About Unexplained Phenomena Since 1965

Ultra-Terrestrials Are Here Screwing With Our Minds

Alien Abduction and Mind Control

MIB - Zombie Love Fest

UFO REVIEW SPECIAL #1

FEATURES

4 ULTRA-TERRESTRIALS ARE HERE SCREWING WITH OUR MINDS - BY TIMOTHY GREEN BECKLEY

14 MIND MANIPULATION - THE NEW UFO TERROR TACTIC - BY TIMOTHY GREEN BECKLEY

30 MESMERIZED FROM ABOVE - BY TIMOTHY GREEN BECKLEY

36 CRIMES AND OTHER EVIL DEEDS OF THE ULTRA-TERRESTRIALS - BY TIMOTHY GREEN BECKLEY

48 ALIEN ABDUCTION AND MIND CONTROL - ARE MERE MORTALS TO BLAME? BY SEAN CASTEEL

56 SHADOW UNIVERSE OF ALIEN THOUGHT CONTROL - BY SEAN CASTEEL

68 RITUAL MAGIC, MIND CONTROL AND THE UFO PHENOMENON - BY ADAM GORIGHTLY

84 MIB - ZOMBIE LOVE FEST - BY TIMOTHY GREEN BECKLEY

92 MIND CONTROL AND THE WOMAN IN BLACK BY NICK REDFERN

100 MIND CONTROLLED MEN IN BLACK BY TIM R. SWARTZ

112 THE PHYSICAL AND SPIRITUAL INFLUENCE OF THE ULTRA-TERRESTRIALS BY TIM R. SWARTZ

SPECIAL REPORTS - 3 Is There an Alien Mind Control Program?, 29 The Salvation of the Soul, 35 The Alien Mind Control Invasion, 96 The Family and Alien Mind Control, 110 Comments From Musician Tom Delonge, 129 For The Control of Humankind's Minds

Copyright © 2016 by Timothy Green Beckley,
All Rights Reserved.
DBA UFO Review, Inner Light - Global Communications
mrufo8@hotmail.com
Global Communications
Box 753, New Brunswick, NJ 08903
Hotline 732 602-3407
YouTube Channel, Mr UFOs Secret Files.
Exploring the Bizarre, KCORradio.com
Free Subscription www.ConspiracyJournal.com
www.TeslaSecretLab.com

A MESSAGE FROM MR. UFO, TIMOTHY GREEN BECKLEY

Timothy Green Beckley

BE FOREWARNED THAT YOU are holding a bold new publication in your hand, a thought provoking one – and the only printed publication now available in North America on the UFO mystery.

Years of research have indicated that the UFO field is divided into many diverse camps. One of the great controversial debating points is focused on the Ultra-Terrestrials' state of mind – are they here to lead us toward a more utopian society or breathing down our necks for the purpose of domination? Do they want to free up our thinking, or boldly, coldly process our souls?

There are, of course, two sides to every coin, and, as we flip the cosmic doubloon, it seems to be landing frequently on the side of negativity. Our probe into this fascinating realm of the paranormal indicates that the Ultra-Terrestrials, as we call them (as we cannot assuredly identify the "aliens" point(s) of origin), have the ability to mesmerize and hypnotize and put us under their mental influence. They are akin to what in the occult realm we would identify as "psychic vampires," harvesters of our spirits and psyches.

In "Project Alien Mind Control," we cover as much territory as is humanly possible in our efforts to rip away the curtain of confusion and global secrecy. If even a fraction of this material is literally, provably accurate, then we can see why the "powers that be" would not want the public to know the ultimate truth – as the ruling class would finally be just as powerless as everyone else in the lower strata of society, equally unable to protect and defend themselves and their families. If there is a menace in the sky, shouldn't we know about it? Or should we be kept in ignorance as we have been for centuries? And could it possibly be that there are even some among us who have traded their allegiance for a pot of cosmic gold, in order to support the "other side"?

We are looking to put out a new UFO REVIEW SPECIAL at least three times a year, covering the many diverse aspects of UFOlogy. The most convenient and economical format would seem to be a large format, such as this, which is sturdy and well-bound to be preserved by collectors. Over the years as editor/publisher of UFO Review, UFO Universe and other paranormal publications, I have attracted some of the best, most capable researchers/writers and we welcome them onboard once again to share with you all the wonderful, suspense-inducing information at our disposal. We also welcome your feedback and support.

Tim –

Follow Us on **YouTube.com** - 100 Plus Video Interviews.
Search For: *Mr UFOs Secret Files* - And Please Subscribe!

YOUR REPORTS AND FEEDBACK ARE WELCOME
Box 753
New Brunswick, NJ 08903
mrufo8@hotmail.com
www.conspiracyjournal.com

PROJECT ALIEN MIND CONTROL -- UFO REVIEW SPECIAL

ACCORDING to researcher Milton L. Scott, at times the popular 1960s television show, "The Invaders," starring Roy Thinnes, seems to be just "a bit more than a concoction of a science fiction writer's vivid imagination; the kidnappings, murders and sabotage being done by David Vincent's adversaries with the opposable pinkies are the same things being done by their true-to-life counterparts." Or so says Mr. Scott, a Philadelphia-based theorist who was known to release "position papers" to his peers.

Furthermore, Scott points out that the difference between the television invaders and the real aliens is that there are no funny looking fingers to make them easy to spot. Thus, in order to carry on their various acts of while on Earth, it is necessary for them to "resemble us as closely as possible." In order to do this, they need not "involve themselves" with using some fantastic hypno-screen that "clouds" our minds to "their true gruesome appearance," because they are no more gruesome looking than Chinese, Japanese, Vietnamese or Ainu.

Because of their Earthling-like appearance, they are able to carry out various acts of "espionage" without being detected. How does a nation wage an undeclared war with yet-to-be-invented weapons against an enemy who is not supposed to exist? Milton Scott speculates: "You might start off by alerting the nation's power complexes to the ever-present danger of sudden blackouts and advising those stations to close each and every switch within reach when they detect a gigantic surge of power racing down the lines from an unknown source."

Or: "You might make noble-sounding pronouncements of peace and friendship to the world – hoping that whoever is listening outside our civilization believes it. You could sign treaties among nations to ban wars in outer space; clutching at the powdery straw contactees have left to us in hopes that flying saucers invading our skies really are big brother-type angels who shed tears over our savage nature.

"You could even build giant radio telescopes to send messages beaming across space: 'We are really nice fellows. We can't hurt you. We only hurt each other. Don't hurt us.'"

Scott asks: "Then what do you do when the blackouts keep occurring and the deaths and the kidnappings continue to mount?

"You could explode nuclear bombs high in the atmosphere in the hope that the radiation will disrupt the machinery of the saucers or even kill their occupants. You could even test your theory by having the bomb explode in the vicinity of a satellite – like the Transit 4-B satellite – and when the satellite suddenly stops sending signals, you could congratulate yourselves on a theory well proved. Then, what do you do when the satellite suddenly comes back to life FIVE YEARS LATER – and starts broadcasting again?"

Obviously, Scott is convinced that the UFOs are here on a non-peaceful mission. We asked him how he reached this important conclusion. His answer was as follows:

"For years, the public has been fed false information from both the government and newspapers who scoffed at anyone who dared to report a flying saucer. It's gotten to the point that the Air Force and the CIA can expect more information from a Martian than they can from John Doe. Ol' John just won't tell anybody anything.

PSYCHOLOGICAL WARFARE

"That's where my tale begins: the first stages of the war that the flying saucer occupants have been waging against us have been psychological. They have spread confusion, fear and doubt from one corner of the globe to the other in order to keep their movements and their purpose a secret until they are ready to make their move. It's a fantastic tale of ghosts, ESP, thought control, liars, dupes and murder.

"The most important battle in the war of the worlds was waged and won in the minds of the people. If there can be one glaring fault on our part that led to our defeat, it was the view that we were the supreme result of billions of years of a thing called evolution – that we were the only intelligent beings in the universe.

"Our scientists, philosophers and clergy boosted our egos by telling us, endlessly, what great works of God we were – so complex (and so stupid) that there couldn't possibly be anyone else as grand and as wonderful as we were. It was a perfect setup, and the characters from the flying saucers exploited it to the fullest extent: they made a few flights over villages, country sides, swamps and cities to shake up the public and drive a wedge between belief in what the government says and what our own eyes say."

In order to keep their mission a secret and make reporting UFOs look like the work of idiots, Scott claims that they used ships of varying shapes, sizes, colors and methods of propulsion to spread confusion among the few investigators. They even used an effect that produces a number of images from a few actual saucers so that the viewers would think there were whole fleets of saucers tooling about the skies. Thus the subject of flying saucers soon became a tiling for disbelief and tired old jokes.

Scott contends that the hundreds of little men, gods, spacemen, winged monsters, surplus Atlantean biplanes and talk of the UFOs being from the inner Earth, a fifth dimension, an antimatter universe, etc., was nothing more than lies and false leads, implanted in gullible earthly minds by the aliens. In reality we were lulled to sleep while more land was taken. We nodded and dreamed while more men and materials from other worlds were flown in. We giggled as things rushed rapidly toward a point of no return. The government refused to believe the abundance of evidence before its eyes until it was too late.

Adamski and all the other contactees, Scott says, did have real enough experiences, but they were selected for their gullibility, and they wrote books that were just as naïve and as gullible as they were. The books got the large heehaw from the public that the aliens had expected, and the case for flying saucers was laughed into obscurity for ten more years while the aliens went about their plans uninterrupted.

If, as Milton Scott says, the aliens' purpose for being here is other than peaceful, and they look almost exactly like us, how then can they be identified? Maybe in the scientific analysis of a "suspected" alien once he has been captured.

"Perhaps the answer is in the chemical balances of the body or in the theory that the little DNA molecules only have a limited number of types to choose from among earthlings."

Interesting theory? So much so that upon hearing of Mr. Scott's opinions many months later, Dr. Edward U. Condon, of the ill-famed University of Colorado UFO study, requested that we send reproductions to him of several newspaper columns which had carried these ideas.

PROJECT ALIEN MIND CONTROL -- UFO REVIEW SPECIAL

UFO researcher Milton L. Scott says that in order to keep their mission a secret and make reporting UFOs look like the work of idiots, extraterrestrials use ships of varying shapes, sizes, colors and methods of propulsion to spread confusion among investigators. **Art By Carol Ann Rodriguez**

PROJECT ALIEN MIND CONTROL -- UFO REVIEW SPECIAL

UFO DIVERSIONS - SEEK TO FIND!

In harmony with many of the opinions expressed by Mr. Milton Scott is another famed UFO investigator who we need to bring into the conversation, the late John A. Keel. Besides being one of America's foremost authorities on flying saucers, Mr. Keel had a long history of objective scientific study of ether phenomena. He was a reporter for decades and authored several bestselling books dealing with both offbeat and more conservative topics.

Commenting on the various diversions inherent in the UFO enigma, Keel told us before his passing that: "From 1897 on it has been a common practice for the UFOs to leave behind ordinary debris such as newspapers, pieces of metal, articles of ordinary clothing, mundane chemicals, etc. Investigators who had discovered such items have often been led to believe that the whole incident was a human hoax or prank of some kind. It is also quite common to find ordinary tire tracks in inaccessible fields where the landings have been reported."

Keel warned us that we should not permit ourselves to be misled by these "negative factors." Keel points out that even in these cases a thorough and investigation should be made.

"We have discovered that a multiple grouping of these negative factors often leads to positive proof that a UFO event DID OCCUR."

Other odd factors inherent in UFO contacts are that "ancient Greek is often employed by the UFO occupants. Greek names and phrases are frequently used for their nonexistent planets. Many of the entities adopt Greek nouns as their personal names. The witnesses very rarely realize this or understand it. Prepare yourself by obtaining and studying a book on Greek mythology."

Keel also suggested that we should also study "our own techniques for psychological warfare, since they are often by employed by the UFOs."

Diversionary landings or seemingly important incidents frequently are staged a few miles from an area where a truly significant UFO activity is taking place. The diversion wins all of our attention and publicity and the important activity goes unnoticed.

Like Scott, Mr. Keel informed us that we should discard all preconceptions.

"You must learn to accept only the correlative evidence and ignore the assorted speculations which have dominated UFOlogy. We are interested only in hard facts. All of these facts indicate that we are dealing with an environmental phenomenon, but that we have been misled into believing the extraterrestrial thesis."

Thus, unlike Milton Scott, John Keel was convinced that the flying saucers, although very real, ARE NOT from other planets.

"So long as we accepted the ET concept, the phenomenon and its source was safe and free from interference. Deliberate hoaxes were executed to sustain skepticism and convince government agencies that the phenomenon was 'non-real.' The UFO buffer was convinced of the ET thesis, which was unacceptable to both the general public and the scientific community. And by loudly advocating it, they succeeded in heaping ridicule upon the subject. Thus the UFO source was able to operate unhindered for decades."

HALLUCINATORY EFFECTS

UFO believers usually rebel at any suggestion that the UFO phenomenon may be hallucinatory or psychological. However, Keel pointed out: "In the past three years many psychological factors have been discovered, and various groups of psychologists and psychiatrists are now actively engaged in UFO research. Unfortunately, very few UFOlogists are trained or equipped to understand or even to investigate the underlying psychological factors. You should read at least on good book on psychiatry and/or psychology."

As far as the contact stories are concerned, Keel told us that "at least some of these cases in the past three years have proven to be hallucinations because it seems that the effects were produced in the witnesses' minds by an exterior influence. These effects are similar to hypnosis. While the witnesses' bodies undergo one sequence or experience, false memories of another sequence of experiences are planted in their minds.

"Frequently, the true (but forgotten) experience surfaces from the witness's subconscious later on in the form of a dream or nightmare. We cannot outline the whole process here, but it must be considered as a very important factor in many cases."

PROJECT ALIEN MIND CONTROL -- UFO REVIEW SPECIAL

IMPORTANT FACTORS IN UFO SIGHTINGS

Some of the important factors to look for in UFO sightings, according to Mr. Keel, include:

"EMOTIONAL REACTIONS – In low-level sightings, auto pursuits, etc., the emotional and psychological responses of the witnesses are extremely important. Get them to explain in detail how they felt immediately before, during and after the sighting. Did they suffer fear, nausea and dizziness? Did they have unusual dreams afterward? In some cases, these reactions are more important than the sighting itself.

"SOUNDS – The sounds accompanying the objects can be of great importance. Many of these sounds have proven to be mental in nature. That is, they were not audible movements of air but were electrical responses in the brains of the observers. Beeping sounds frequently indicate that the witness was subjected to an unconscious experience. Such witnesses may find that they are unable to explain lapses of time or geographical transfers during such sightings. Such witnesses should be examined by a qualified psychiatrist whenever possible.

"EYE BURN – Witnesses who suffer from burned or inflamed eyes after viewing a UFO should be examined immediately by a professional doctor and a full medical report should be obtained. In those cases involving 'eye burn' weeks or months previous to the investigation, the investigator should get the witness to draw up a full statement explaining in full the reactions suffered. Medical documentation is most important.

"DREAMS – Many witnesses suffer unusual nightmares weeks before their UFO sighting. Others have strange nightmares for weeks afterward. These dreams are important, and you should obtain full descriptions of them. Some witnesses begin to have prophetic dreams after their UFO experience.

"In landing cases, when definite marks are found on the ground, they should be photographed and measurements carefully made. For the past 20 years, hundreds of landings have been neglected even though the markings are always similar in size and formation. If we had collected and documented photos of all these landings, we would now have an impressive body of correlative evidence.

"In further investigating important sightings, landings and contact experiences, under no circumstances should any witness be hypnotized by anyone other than a qualified psychiatrist. Amateur hypnotists have ruined several important cases in recent years."

MEN IN BLACK

During this same period which John Keel speaks of, there has been an increasing number of cases which involve the MIB, or Men In Black. These strange individuals have been known to warn UFO witnesses not to reveal what they have seen long before the case is ever made public.

Keel commented on the activities of these MIB, pointing out that many different investigators in "flap" areas have now had confirmatory experiences with the MIB and only a small percentage of these cases have been published.

There are several different types of MIB. One group appears to be more psychic or hallucinatory than real. They appear and disappear suddenly in bedrooms; the witnesses often experience paralysis or a sudden rise in temperature while in the presence of the MIB. We now have dozens of such cases in our files.

Another type common throughout the U.S. is represented by men who travel in pairs. The same description is always given. One man is tall, blond (usually has a crew cut), has a fair complexion and seems to be a Scandinavian. His companion is shorter, with angular features and a dark olive complexion. The blond usually does the talking while the other remains in the background. There seem to be several identical pairs of these individuals operating simultaneously in several states.

Other types of MIB include men with Asian features, dark complexions, slight stature and heavy indefinable accent. These men sometimes pose as salesmen or some other form of business occupation that normally requires a suit and tie.

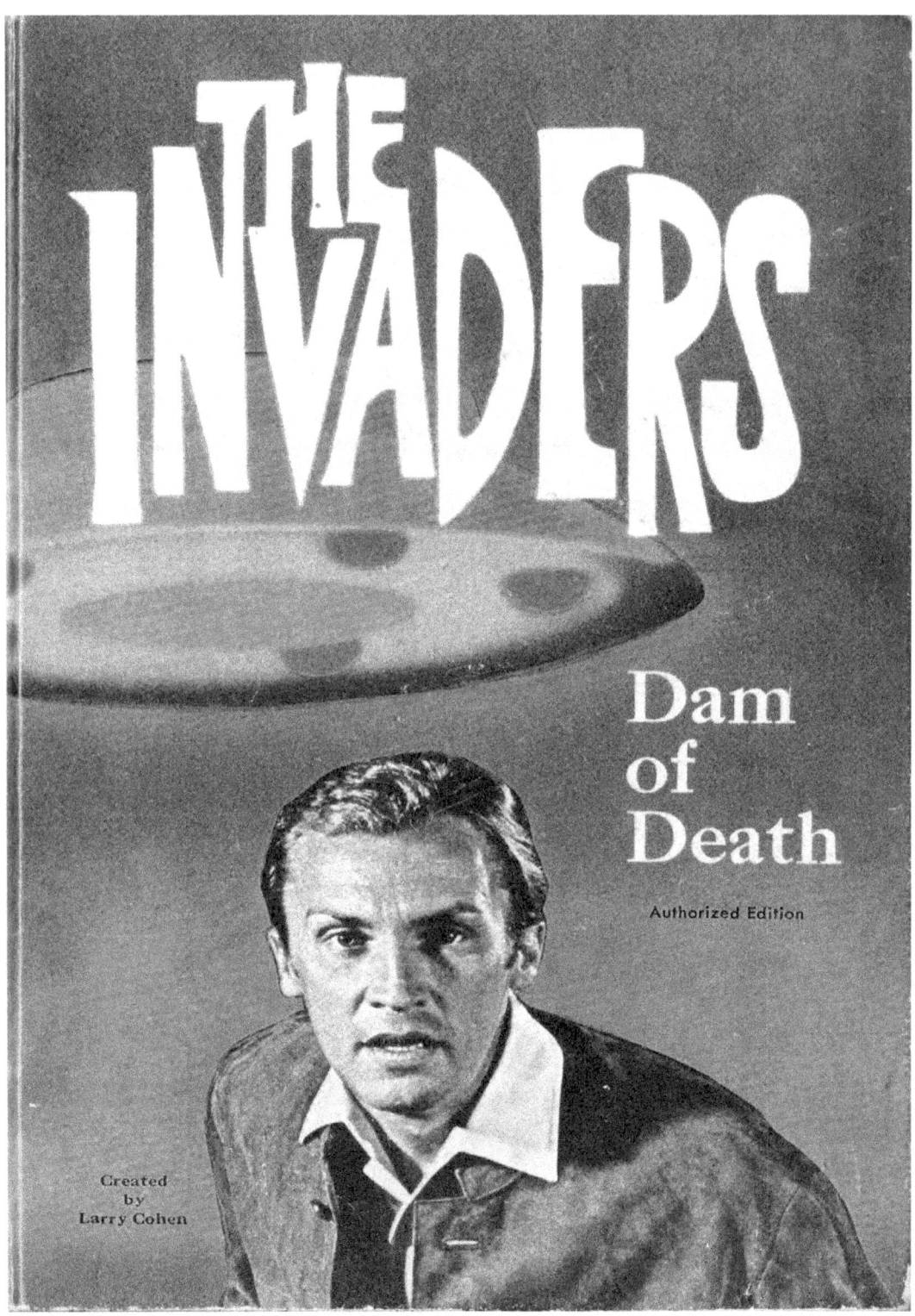

The TV series **The Invaders** was closer to being true than most viewers realized.

PROJECT ALIEN MIND CONTROL -- UFO REVIEW SPECIAL

THERE are mounting indications that UFOs have a long-term plan of operation in store for Earth and its inhabitants. Data, meticulously collected in a worldwide research effort, would seem to support that stunning theory.

UFO literature is filled with hundreds of cases in which unsuspecting observers have been subjected to continuous harassments following an encounter with a flying saucer. Many times the witness finds his home plagued by a host of inexplicable phenomena. In other cases, eerie, mechanical-sounding voices, purporting to be "messages" from an alien source, begin emanating from their radios, TV sets or telephones. In addition, mysterious strangers dressed in dark clothing, commonly referred to as the Men In Black, or MIB, visit the often confused eyewitness and warn them not to speak about their sighting to anyone.

Many observers, however, endure far more harrowing experiences than these. As terrifying as these incidents may seem, they cannot be compared to the instances which appear to be actual cases of "UFO possession."

Often, while interviewing a UFO witness or contactee, I find myself face-to-face with an individual who is convinced he is slowly – but surely – losing touch with reality. Having come that close to the unknown, the individual feels his very existence is being threatened by an alien force bent on gaining total control of his body and soul.

Some witnesses persist in believing that they are being "haunted" day and night by an invisible specter whose main objective is to capture the witness's free will and make them the "property" of someone – or something – else.

Cases of UFO possession are often quite common! Yet very little is known about it because of the scarcity of research into the subject. Investigators have remained extremely cautious about digging too deeply into this particular area. Their hesitancy, however, may be justified.

An exhaustive study of my own shows that accounts of UFO possession are almost always identical. Frightfully so! The following patterns have emerged, again and again:

*** After a close encounter with a UFO, the eyewitness goes through a period of anxiety during which he is unable to consciously remember certain aspects of the incident.

PROJECT ALIEN MIND CONTROL -- UFO REVIEW SPECIAL

*** Within months – sometimes weeks or even days – the personality of the observer actually changes. Eventually the observer's personality may alter to the point where he finds it impossible to get along with coworkers, close friends or even family. Personal tragedy seems to strike many of those who have had ground level encounters with UFOs. Much could be written about individuals whose entire personal world crumbles around them following such an experience.

*** In some cases, the eyewitness discovers he has developed certain "gifts" or abilities. Though they may appear to be beneficial at first, too frequently this is not the case. Among these unusual abilities are extraordinary powers of ESP, precognition or psychokinesis. In addition, a heightened intelligence level or an unusual increase in physical strength may be noticed. Such peculiarities will often manifest themselves shortly before a person is about to be possessed. Shortly after this, he may begin slipping into a "trance," during which it appears as if an alien intelligence has "taken over" his body and is using his brain.

It was during my in-depth investigation of an extensive UFO wave in the U.S. Southwest that I met Simon Swagger, a tall, slimly-built man in his mid-20s. (Because of the seriousness and the possible repercussions this may cause, we have decided to change the names of those individuals involved.)

Simon's story is one of the most believable accounts of alien possession that I have ever heard. And I'm convinced it is not a hoax.

During the course of three rather lengthy conversations with Simon, I felt I learned much about him. Like so many other American boys, he spent his teenage years playing baseball, listening to music and chasing girls. Simon never paid close attention to his schoolwork, with the result that his grades were "just average." Nevertheless, he was well liked by his classmates and also managed to get along amicably with his elders.

Now, at 25, this same "average young man" feels destitute, as if he doesn't have a friend in the world. Nearly a total recluse, he shuns any activity which might expose him to public scrutiny. He is divorced from his wife of four years and has quit or been fired from numerous jobs.

Of course, these radical changes in his life did not occur overnight but rather were a painfully slow period of moral and physical deterioration.

Simon was more than willing to tell me the details of his ordeal. As we talked, it became apparent that he was anxious to get the matter off his chest. The problem had obviously been weighing him down for too many years.

"For the longest time I thought I was going insane," Simon said. "Often my best friends would accuse me of behaving irrationally, and I wouldn't have a clue about what they were referring to. My mind, on those occasions, was an absolute blank. I found myself going to doctors and psychiatrists, but even they couldn't offer me an explanation that could account for these amnesia attacks."

FIRST THE THUNDER AND THEN AN OMINOUS ENCOUNTER

Whatever the cause of his trouble, it was obvious that it was rooted in an eerie confrontation with a visitor from outer space! The event took place on a Friday night in August 1967. At the time, Simon lived with his parents on a rather secluded ranch near Waco, Texas, which was surrounded by trees, dense thickets and bramble. Here is his personal account of what happened on that fateful summer evening:

"The weather had been unbearably hot all day, with temperatures soaring into the 90s. I got permission from my folks to spend the night outdoors, camped in back of our ranch house with a couple of friends.

"We set up a makeshift shelter, turned on a portable radio and proceeded to shoot the breeze. The sky was as clear as I'd ever seen it, with stars twinkling against a background of absolute blackness.

"Around 10 P.M., the air began to gradually get cooler. In the distance we could hear an occasional rumble of thunder, and once in while the sky would light up with a flash of lightning. It was a great sight."

Unfortunately, the beauty of the night was short-lived. It was shattered less than two hours later.

"Shortly after midnight, we lowered the flame of our kerosene lantern and retired," Simon Swagger continued, a slight trace of tension building in his voice. "Immediately I turned over and closed my eyes. Before long, however, a peculiar high-pitched whine woke me up. The nearest I can come to describing this would be to say it sounded like a million bees buzzing."

Sitting up, Simon peered into the darkness and saw nothing. With a few moments, however, he managed to pinpoint the source of the noise. It was coming from the woods near the ranch. With his curiosity now aroused, Simon decided to investigate.

"I didn't want to wake up my friends, so I tiptoed over to the area, hoping to catch a glimpse of whatever was causing the noise. I recall wandering aimlessly farther and farther away from our backyard camp, as if I was being pulled by an invisible rope. All around me, the whine continued to grow in intensity until finally it encircled me on all sides."

At this point, Simon sighted his first UFO.

"Up ahead of me, between the trees and bushes, was a glowing light the size of a basketball. As I approached to within 25 feet of it, I could see the light was actually a pulsating sphere."

In an attempt to block out the loud, irritating noise that continued to grow in intensity, Simon put his hands over his ears. This had little effect, however.

"My head began to swim, and my eyes started to water. Next thing I knew, I was on my hands and knees – somehow I must have fallen without realizing it – crawling on the ground, trying to get back to the safety of my friends."

He was unsuccessful.

Upon "coming to," Simon found himself in his parents' living room. His head was pounding from "the worst headache I've ever experienced." Standing around him were his mother and father and his two friends.

Simon says he found it difficult to understand what they were trying to tell him.

"It was as if they were talking to a complete stranger," he said. "I had, for all intents and purposes, lost my identity. I had no idea who I was or where I was."

While he tried to calm his nerves and gather his thoughts, Simon's friends filled him in on what had happened.

"They said they had suddenly been awakened by a brilliant flash off in the woods. They noticed that I wasn't in my sleeping bag, nor did they see me nearby, and they became worried. Considering all the possibilities, they felt I might have wandered off in my sleep and fallen into one of the many ravines in the area," Simon said.

Using a flashlight to guide them through the underbrush, Simon's friends began calling out his name. Their worry grew into fear because he did not respond to their cries.

Five minutes later, their search ended when they found Simon stretched out on the ground face down.

"Lifting me to my feet, they explained how I seemed to be in another world, dazed and looking right through them. My eyes, they claimed, were rolled back in their sockets and my skin had turned as white as a sheet. In addition, they said my flesh felt ice cold, like that of a corpse."

On the way back to the house, they noticed something else. Simon's head had swollen like a balloon. His forehead appeared enlarged and extended several inches beyond normal.

"It was 'puffed up,' as if I'd been stung by a mass of bees."

This condition rapidly disappeared and Simon's head returned to normal by the time the three boys reached the safety of his parents' quiet ranch house.

For weeks afterward, Simon felt worn out, "as if I'd been drained of all my energy." He found it extremely difficult to concentrate long enough to do even the most mundane chores. All he could do was mope around the house and he spent a good portion of the time sleeping.

As the months went by, Simon regained his strength. However, even as he returned to normal physically, he couldn't help but wonder about what had really happened on that late summer night.

"My friends came up with a rather logical explanation. They concluded that I'd been walking in my sleep – I'd never done that before, to my knowledge – and that a thunderstorm had come up in the middle of the night and I had barely missed being struck by lightning. They figured a bolt had struck near where I stood, and, after traveling over the surface of the ground, had reached me. Along the way, the lightning must have lost a great deal of force. Otherwise, they theorized, I would surely have been instantly killed."

Though their explanation seemed reasonable, Simon couldn't shake the persistent feeling that a lot more was involved.

"I recalled a bright light, dizzy spells, headaches, and fainting spells. And a strange buzzing that literally ran through my skull."

He knew there had to be another answer – even if it was an unpleasant one.

After several years had passed, Simon became engaged to and later married his high school sweetheart, Irene.

"After we got married, I took a job as a ranch hand near Calvert, Texas. And though the week was tiring, it paid pretty well. Each week, I was able to put some money in the bank, figuring someday I would have enough saved to buy a small place of our own and perhaps even start a small cattle business."

Since that night in back of his parents' house, Simon suffered both mentally and physically. The dizzy spells, headaches and fainting became common.

"I'd be seated at the kitchen table and all of a sudden my wife would be applying cold compresses to my forehead. I'd pass right out reading the newspaper or eating."

Gradually his condition deteriorated. During this difficult period which followed his UFO experience, Simon became keenly fascinated with science and began reading books on physics and engineering, subjects in which he had never before shown even a mild interest.

"It was as if I were furthering my education," he said. "I didn't know why I found these topics so fascinating. My mind seemed to be developing – expanding – at a rapid clip."

Coinciding with this heightened curiosity and intelligence, Simon found himself growing extremely moody. As the months passed, and after discussing his suspicions with his wife, that ufonauts were trying to control him, it became more difficult for Simon to be around other people – including his wife, parents and coworkers.

"I had a hard time keeping my thoughts together."

He started showing up late for work and then not showing up at all. Finally, he quit, not wanting to wait until he was fired. A string of lesser paying jobs followed, but they all ended the same way. Then things went from bad to worse.

"My mind was incapable of thinking straight. It was always a million miles away, toying with some advanced mathematical formula or scientific equation. The funny part of all this was that I still didn't know the reason why I was so hung up on these things. After all, I wasn't a scientist or an engineer, just a simple country boy."

During this period, personal tragedy struck the Swaggers. Their year-old son suddenly died. Doctors concluded that the infant had succumbed to a cerebral hemorrhage. In early 1973, Simon's wife left him and filed for divorce. One of the reasons she gave was that she felt the boy's death was somehow related to Simon's condition. She felt that the UFO issue had broken up their previously happy marriage. This same pattern is often repeated as UFO witnesses have found their formerly normal lives turned into nightmares.

Simon didn't even bother to contest the divorce action.

"Even though I loved Irene dearly, she didn't matter that much to me anymore. It was as though I had a special mission on Earth. It was 'beyond me' to lead an ordinary existence."

Irene's decision to leave came after Simon's second encounter with mysterious unidentified objects. Not knowing what to expect – or what her husband was capable of doing – she decided to leave.

"Again, I must tell you what happened as seen through another person's eyes. My mind is almost a total blank when it comes to the events of that night."

Simon and his wife were driving home from Belmont, Texas, where they had spent the evening with relatives.

"It was around 1:30 A.M., and I was speeding along the darkened back roads to avoid traffic, when suddenly a large, yellowish ball of fire appeared on the road ahead. Immediately I slammed on the brakes because otherwise I would have collided head-on with the object."

The UFO slowly lifted from the road a few feet above the pavement and began drifting toward the side of the road. About 30 seconds passed before it stopped and hovered next to a grove of trees. It was then that a frightened Simon Swagger insists he was directed, as if by magic, to leave his car and walk toward the UFO, which now remained stationary. Just as in his first UFO experience, the nighttime air was now filled with an eerie, loud whine, similar to a shrill scream.

"My wife pleaded with me not to leave the car, but I was no longer in control of my movements. It was as if my body was being made to react, pulling me in the direction 'they' wanted."

Walking toward the light, Simon says he heard a voice inside his head. This "inner voice" demanded that he walk straight ahead and not look back.

Meanwhile, inside the parked car, Irene Swagger was almost hysterical.

"She considered going for help but was afraid the police might think she was daffy," Simon said. "So, in desperation, and because there wasn't anything else to do, she decided to 'sit tight,' hoping I would return soon."

When he did, havoc followed.

"Somehow, I wound up back in my car. Opening the car door, my wife says I looked like a 'monster' – that's exactly the way she put it. My face was more alien in appearance than human. My features had changed grotesquely, eyes bulging out of their sockets."

She compared his face to the creation of a master makeup artist on the set of a science fiction movie. Shaking nervously, Mrs. Swagger tried to get Simon to climb into the backseat where he could lie down and remain calm while she drove to the nearest hospital. Irene thought a wild beast or perhaps a poisonous snake had attacked her husband. Instead of complying with her wishes, Simon pushed her aside with a "violent shove" that sent her sprawling against the opposite door. Simon slid into the driver's seat and grabbed the steering wheel in a rage.

"Supposedly I was talking incoherently, as if in a trance."

When he gripped the wheel, it bent out of shape like it was made of putty. Within a minute of this remarkable feat – one that would require extraordinary strength – Simon slumped against the dashboard with his eyes shut and his forehead dripping perspiration.

To Simon, it was all a dream. "I don't remember a damn thing after leaving the car and hearing the hypnotic sounding voice and seeing the lighted object. If it wasn't for the steering wheel being twisted, I'd say my wife probably made up the whole crazy story."

Since his second meeting with a UFO, Simon feels more strongly than ever he is being influenced by alien beings. Since his last encounter with ufonauts, Simon Swagger's life has stabilized somewhat. He has learned to cope with the "force" trying to control him. At this time, this "average student" is on the threshold of obtaining a degree in electrical engineering!

THE CIA VERSUS "THE SPACEMEN"

While Simon's narrative is intriguing in itself, he is by no means the only person to have been selected to receive such "special" treatment at the hands of ufonauts. Even high-ranking government officials have received "communications" and been "manipulated."

Somewhere in a locked file cabinet, hidden in some obscure office in the Pentagon, is a two-inch thick file that contains perhaps the best-documented UFO possession case of the decade. The episode actually involves an Air Force officer, the Office of Naval Intelligence and the CIA.

For a long time, this manila folder was closely guarded – stamped "Top Secret." Its contents were finally leaked to an enterprising scriptwriter, Robert Emenegger, on assignment from Sandler Institutional Films, producers of a syndicated documentary on UFOs. The source of this "leak" was, surprisingly enough, Lt. Col. Robert Friend, USAF, former head of Project Blue Book and well-known "staff debunker" for the government.

Now long retired, Friend seems to have done an "about-face" on the question of UFOs. Not only does he think they exist, but he also seems to give serious consideration to the even more puzzling UFO contactee cases.

PROJECT ALIEN MIND CONTROL -- UFO REVIEW SPECIAL

A most revealing interview with Friend appears in the book "UFOs, Past, Present and Future." In this interview, the former Blue Book spokesman describes a case which contains all the typical elements of a "UFO Possession."

While head of the Air Force's UFO project, Friend says he was informed, as a "matter of courtesy," that a well-respected Rear Admiral was especially interested in a woman living in Maine who claimed to be receiving highly advanced and technologically correct information from extraterrestrial beings. These entities were said to contact her while she sat in a trancelike state. The admiral, with the approval of the Air Force, sent two of his most responsible and trusted men to investigate.

Relaxing in a chair before them, the woman expressed her willingness to answer any questions they might have. At this point, she no longer seemed to have control of her physical self. Her body was ostensibly "taken over" by members of an intergalactic organization referred to as the "Universal Association of Planets."

A few minutes into this unprecedented "conversation," one of the officers present, a Navy commander, was told that further questions would be directed through him. The officer was instructed to hold a pen lying on a nearby table. The "spaceman" then took control of his hand and proceeded to respond to questions through a process known in parapsychological circles as "automatic writing."

Colonel Friend notes that news of this highly provocative experiment reached Washington almost before the men returned. Top officials at the Central Intelligence Agency also heard about the episode and demanded to know more. It was Friend's duty to find out what he could.

"CAN WE SEE A SPACESHIP?"

"It was in 1959," he told researcher/scriptwriter Emenegger, "when I was invited to attend a meeting in the security section of a government building in Washington. I was briefed on an experiment that had been conducted with this same Navy commander before a group of CIA members and military personnel. It was described how, after going into a trance, the commander contacted a supposed extraterrestrial being. Several questions were put to him, and answers came back, such as 'Do you favor any government, group or race?' The answer was 'No.' 'Can we see a spaceship?' The commander, still in a trance, told the group to go to the window and they'd have proof. The group went to the window, where they supposedly observed a UFO. I was told that when a call was made for a radar confirmation, the tower reported that that particular quadrant of the sky was blanked out on radar at that time."

Friend says that after being briefed on all the details he asked if the officer could attempt a contact for him personally. While he watched, the commander went into a deep trance.

"Questions were put to him, and he printed the answers in rather large letters, using rapid but jerky motions very unlike his natural handwriting. During the course of the questioning, we were told the names of some of the so-called extraterrestrials. One was 'Crill,' another 'Alomar,' and another 'Affa,' purportedly from the planet Uranus."

The former head of Blue Book admits that he was puzzled.

"All those involved were found to be highly credible and responsible professional government men," Friend affirmed.

After turning in his report, Friend was told by a superior to forget the entire affair. He was informed that the CIA was making their own study, and therefore the Air Force was being instructed to "lay off."

What was his reaction to this command? As might be expected, it was a military one.

"Well, when a general tells a colonel to forget it - you forget it!"

Friend later discovered that every witness present in that government office on the day the Navy officer went into a trance was relocated or transferred to other duty.

"To this day," concludes the ex-Air Force officer, "it's an unresolved incident to me. I just don't know what to make of it. It seems totally unique in all my experience with investigations of UFOs."

Had he cooperated to any degree with civilians, Colonel Friend probably wouldn't have been so awed with this case. For many years, private organizations have patiently gathered and investigated similar cases. Indeed, whole sects have been founded based on similar "trance" messages.

THE SILVER-GARBED "VENUSIANS" AND THE "MENTAL CONTACTEES"

There are hundreds of so-called "mental contactees" who claim to receive information and data of a highly advanced scientific and philosophical nature. In fact, during the 1950s and 60s, this method of communication with UFOs occupants (better known as "channeling") became so popular that entities calling themselves "Ashtar," "Agar" and "Monka" were heard from daily somewhere in the world. As far back as the 1920s, the "I AM" religious movement gathered a tremendous number of supporters. Their entire doctrine was derived from the messages purportedly delivered through their leader from a "higher" source. And even earlier, around the turn of the century, Madame Blavatsky founded the Theosophical Society. Her "guide" was a long-deceased Tibetan master. Today, Madame Blavatsky might find that her white-robed monk was a silvery-garbed "Venusian." The "source" appears to be the same; only the "messages" have changed.

There is no doubt that this phenomenon is widespread and is by no means limited to the U.S. cases of mind-altering UFO possession seem to be occurring on a global scale and at an alarming rate. There have been reports of entire towns being placed under a strange "spell," with the simultaneous appearance of flying saucers in the area.

A large-scale attempt to invade and seize the minds of human beings occurred on April 19, 1967, when a coastal village on the outskirts of Rio de Janeiro became the target of a strange aerial visitor. For approximately one hour on that day, the hundreds of citizens of Barra de Tijuca, Brazil were literally forced into establishing contact with an unearthly intelligence which quickly subdued every single person in town. The series of disturbing events began at noon when an emergency telephone call reached Dr. Jeronemo Rodrigues Morales, chief physician at Barra de Tijuca's general hospital.

An excited voice explained how a man in his late 60s had fallen unconscious on the beach near town. The caller seemed alarmed because felt certain the man had suffered a heart attack.

Apologizing to his waiting patients, Dr. Morales immediately drove to the scene. Upon arriving, he found the man brushing sand from his clothes. He was standing and quietly talking to a crowd of people who had gathered to offer help.

"I was merely walking about the sand dunes," the man explained. "I had been watching the birds high above the water when suddenly I blacked out."

An on-the-spot examination, conducted in the hospital's old ambulance, ruled out the possibility of a heart attack, and Dr. Morales decided that the man had suffered a mild case of sunstroke. Knowing he was needed back at the hospital, the physician headed back to his waiting patients. Within minutes, however, the ambulance's shortwave radio blurted out the disturbing news that a fisherman had been discovered in shallow water beneath a nearby bridge and was said to be trembling from shock.

Dr. Morales quickly drove to the area and arrived just in time to see the "stricken" fisherman casually drying himself off and inquiring what all the excitement was about. When the doctor explained that he had blacked out, the man seemed insulted.

"I'm not sick," he argued. "I feel perfectly well."

He assured Dr. Morales that he had been tossing his nets into these waters every day for 20 years without any difficulty and would do so for 20 more.

WAS THE ENTIRE TOWN ATTACKED?

Within a short while, Dr. Morales received word of six other "stricken" individuals. All followed the identical pattern: people keeling over, and then reviving themselves without aid, and, after a flurry of excitement, vehemently insisting that "it was absolutely nothing."

The next episode, which occurred a little after 1 P.M., involved a young woman who had been innocently strolling along the beach with her three-year-old child at her side. Suddenly they both "passed out." Because of the child's age, Dr. Morales insisted the youngster be taken to the hospital for an extensive examination. The worried mother readily agreed.

While carrying the young boy into the emergency ward, Dr. Morales happened to glance skyward. High above, glistening in the sun, was a tremendous elongated object—a UFO. He watched as the shiny craft wobbled back and forth. It went through an entire series of gyrations. Several times it dropped lower in the sky, offering a better look at its metallic surface. Then, just as rapidly, it would dart back to its former position high in the clear blue sky.

During lunch, several other physicians and nurses on the hospital staff excitedly commented on their own sightings of a "cigar-shaped" craft which they observed suspended over the town that day since noon.

Coincidental? Most unlikely. Three days later the same craft appeared again. Once more, a number of people dropped unconscious to the ground. During these two days, many other individuals were treated at the hospital for headaches and dizziness, no rational cause being found for their illness. From the evidence we have uncovered, the cause seems apparent.

Often, a UFO witness or contactee is convinced he is slowly – but surely – losing touch with reality. Having come that close to the unknown, the individual feels his very existence is being threatened by an alien force bent on gaining total control of his body and soul.

THE SALVATION OF THE SOUL

COURTESY THE LATE E. BLANCHE PRITCHETT FROM HER SPACE CONTACTS

Give this word to all that will hear and bring cheer to the inhabitants of this planet in its time of the greatest stress and trouble it has ever had, or ever will have in its history.

The war that you are waging is an invisible war. It is a war of minds and thoughts. It is a war wherein the evil poisons of the psycho-polities are used ruthlessly by the oppressors.

It is a word of para-mental tactics designed to implant fear and phobia into the minds of men.

It is a war that all religionists speak of in their pulpits as though it were somewhere far off in the streams of time and there was still time to philosophize about it! It is the war prophesied in every religion upon the Earth today.

It is the battle of the White Brotherhood versus the forces of darkness. To the student, it is the attack upon honor by dishonor. It matters little which study one prefers or which way of thinking one has adopted. It matters greatly that this is it – to the Christian, it is the Battle of Armageddon. To the Buddhist, it is the War of Bodhis.

It is a time for going within. It is a time for the light to begin to shine within you.

MESMERIZED FROM ABOVE

By Timothy Green Beckley

ARE THE UFO INTELLIGENCES USING TELEPATHY TO COMMUNICATE WITH HUMANITY...OR TO CONTROL OUR THOUGHTS?

PROJECT ALIEN MIND CONTROL -- UFO REVIEW SPECIAL

IN the July 1959 issue of the "APRO Bulletin," edited by Carol Lorenzen, one of the most astounding but well-documented contacts of a telepathic type is reported in great detail. It tells of a Mr. Helio Aguiar, who was on his way to Amaralian, Brazil, to get a weapon, a hand revolver, and return it later to his good friend, Captain Leib Leibovitch of the Sixth Regiment. Borrowing the Captain's motorcycle and hoping to take pictures of his nephews who lived in the area, he proceeded on his way.

Noting that it was a most beautiful day, he decided to take one last ride on the Captain's cycle along the marvelous stretch of modern highway which runs for several miles between the sea and palm tree thickets to Itapoan.

As Helio approached the community of Piatan, he took note of "something like a dark smear in the sky just over the ocean." At first, he thought it might be some defect of his vision, but the smear was getting sharp and closing in. At this moment, the engine of the motorcycle stopped. Helio noticed that the smear was a disc, flattened at one of its faces, from where protruded four half-sphere, and on which some dark signs were visible, like symbols.

On the upper portion of the ship was a circular dome or enclosed area. He was not sure whether this was of glass or metal since the sun was shining brightly on it, making it hard to see. Grabbing his camera, which he normally carried with him, he took three photos. While he was doing so, the object made a number of rotations in the air. It was during the process of taking his photos that Helio began to feel a strange force or pressure on his temple and he was growing mentally confused. He recalled later that he received an impression to write something. Shortly thereafter, he completely passed out, apparently while taking a fourth shot of the phenomenon.

When he revived, Helio found himself slumped over his friend's motorcycle with one hand positioned inside his pocket and a pencil in the other. Not taking notice at first, because of his dazed and bewildered condition, he rested under one of the nearby palm trees. After a few minutes, his attention was drawn to a piece of paper in his pocket which bore some unfamiliar words, apparently in his own handwriting, written in Portuguese. It contained the following message, which Helio had written while under the mental control of the UFO which had maneuvered in the sky before him:

"ATOMIC EXPERIMENTS FOR WARLIKE PURPOSES SHALL BE DEFINITELY STOPPED . . . THE EQUILIBRIUM OF THE UNIVERSE IS THREATENED. WE WILL REMAIN VIGILANT AND READY TO INTERFERE."

Before having this experience, Helio had spent considerable time studying New Age topics such as hypnosis, telepathy and metaphysics. It has been suggested that, since he had a good background in this field, the visitors may have found him to be an ideal subject for their communications.

It would be interesting to know if further material has been received through this channel since 1959. Although this is a most unusual account, it is not without confirmation from many other sources.

Years ago, a letter of mine appeared in THE SOUTH AMBOY EVENING NEWS, asking that readers send in their own personal experiences for study and evaluation by our staff. One of the better reports I received in the mail following this letter came from a resident of Perth Amboy, New Jersey, who requested that I not publicly mention her name.

In her letter, she described to me an event which occurred to her and her fiancé, now her husband, in the autumn of 1958. At the time, she was only 15 years old and her boyfriend only two years older. One day they decided to take a ride through nearby Roosevelt Park in Metuchen, New Jersey, which was a favorite spot at the time for teenagers. She estimated that it was about 8:30 P.M., and they were parked by the lake in front of Roosevelt Hospital. She happened to look up at the night sky and noticed, to the left of the hospital, three objects which were hovering above a wooded area. She knew almost at once that they couldn't be planes because they stood still in the sky. The objects were egg-shaped and brilliantly lit.

After some discussion of what they were viewing, the young couple decided to drive toward the object to get a closer look at them. As they did, the UFOs began to move off. They followed them southward on the Garden State Parkway at 60 miles per hour.

At the Perth Amboy exit, the objects turned almost completely around and flew off into another direction. They weren't able to follow them this time as they were unable to leave the Parkway. They had noticed that other people were also looking at the craft and it gave them considerable comfort to know that they weren't losing their sanity.

Most of the time, the three objects traveled in a "V" formation with one leader and two followers. They maintained the same distance from each other, even while turning. The rest of this woman's story is so fascinating and backs up Helio Aguiar's encounter so well that I have decided to quote directly from her letter in order not to change the exact wording of her account:

"All the while I looked at these objects, I had a feeling of someone trying to ask me a question. Not in the usual verbal sense, but sort of like a pressure on my head. And all the while I felt terribly fearful that something was going to happen. I actually fought against this feeling, and, when the object turned to leave, this pressure became less and less and finally disappeared."

HOW "TRUE" ARE THESE MESSAGES FROM AFAR?

The strange pressure felt on the temples, as reported above, is nothing new to UFO and New Age authorities. Henry R. Gallart, in his book, **FROM OTHER WORLDS**, describes how these strange pressures, which lasted over a period of many months, would coincide with his receiving what appeared to be nonverbal messages from highly-evolved beings on other planets. Some of these messages were in the form of stories, some of them worded so that Mr. Gallart believed they may actually have been describing another incarnation he went through on another planet before his present life on Earth. Other material which Gallart received concerned itself with such subjects as war, religion, the atom and sex.

I might point out here that Mr. Gallart was no "kook," but a respected chemical engineer who worked for a large water and power company in California. He was not given to flights of fancy and had even suggested that I place too much value in these accounts.

On the West Coast, a husband-and-wife team, Wes and Jo Nell Bateman, appeared on numerous TV and radio shows and predicted the appearance of UFOs. In fact, some ten days before the historic flap in Michigan, the Batemans told an audience in Santa Monica that saucers would be seen over Ann Arbor.

Their means of receiving this and additional information is through the use of mental control, or what we call telepathy. There are affidavits signed by people of sound occupation and background, ranging from a teacher, educational director, wife, to an active Marine Corps Lt. Colonel, and two civilian pilots. All were witnesses during two nights of UFO sightings over Hollywood which was predicted in advance by Mr. and Mrs. Bateman.

Bateman claimed his first mental contact occurred in 1963, when he heard a voice in his head explain to him that advanced beings from other planets were attempting to make contact before widespread landings could be affected. From that moment on, the Batemans were in almost constant mental contact with the Saucer Intelligences and received important information on the propulsion mechanics of the saucers, the true purposes of the UFO visits to Earth and the reason for the lack of direct physical contact between these visitors and the inhabitants of the Earth.

It has been suggested that the form of communications used in this form of contact may actually be even more advanced than telepathy as we are beginning to know it. Some have even suggested that it is more on the line of mental waves (pure energy in itself) which can even be used to power the aliens' spacecraft.

In Mexico, there has been much UFO activity in which a great many people have apparently made reliable contacts and communicated by telepathy with the pilots of UFOs. In one case, three University of Mexico architecture students say they were taken to the third moon of Jupiter in a flying saucer piloted by seven-foot-tall beings. The journey took only three hours and, during that time and the time they were on the third moon, there was no verbal communication. Instead this was done by means of brain waves or "advanced mental telepathy." The three students claim that the pilots, who looked like the spacemen that George Adamski and others claim to have met (except for their height), were even able to transfer their brain waves into thought forms to maneuver their ship.

A group of 82 scientists in California met to discuss the future of man and his mental capabilities. They generally agreed that it may soon be possible both to build a machine to read a person's brainwaves and to have a "brain-computer link" to enlarge man's intellect. They see these things as being possible within the next several decades. And certainly a group of beings who have been able to travel the dark voids of outer space for ages (as recent archeological evidence indicates) would find it simple to use their brainwaves in such a simple matter as to guide a spaceship or communicate with Earthmen.

THE ALIEN MIND CONTROL INVASION: LOOK, THEY WANTED YOU TO KNOW ABOUT IT.

April 19, 2013 at 2:39 pm

I have been shown the machinations of an alien invasion and have attempted to warn everyone about it. It's not the kind of invasion you would expect because that wouldn't work as well as one you don't see coming. Here's a hint: they are using mind control to take over the planet without even needing to set foot on it. For a three-year period, I have personally witnessed effects of mind control similar to several prominent victims of this same conspiracy.

For some reason, they would like you to know. To this end they have hidden a pattern in the prophetic works of Huxley, Orwell and Phillip K. Dick. This pattern serves to confirm an earlier revelation, regarding the date of "arrival" being between August and September of 2016.

There is a significant amount of additional evidence of mind control in our history. First and foremost, consider the cases of the recent assassinations and assassination attempts from Kennedy to Reagan. Incidentally, I was born on the day John Lennon was assassinated. It's been made clear to me that the MK-ULTRA program is casually related to the Roswell incident. I think it's a Trojan horse, and this "entity" is attempting to use that program as evidence to the world that our government is responsible for mind-controlling everyone.

It also appears that mind control was utilized for the benefit of the Nazis during World War II and that the Angel of Death was actively researching the technology behind it.

Also, just like the Sandy Hook and China Stabbing incidents occurred at nearly the same time with very similar stories, a similar event occurred in the 17th century, in Salem and France. These things are too much to be coincidence. Maybe they are trying to disarm us and blame the government for it at the same time?

Even before that, we seem to have a significant amount of evidence of the use of this technology, going all the way back to Ancient Egypt.

Please wake up!

FROM A FACEBOOK POSTING

PROJECT ALIEN MIND CONTROL -- UFO REVIEW SPECIAL

INDIVIDUALS in the grip of UFO possession often behave irrationally and have even been known to commit criminal acts.

Former NASA Mars mapping expert, Dr. Jacques Vallee, in his third book, *Passport To Magonia*, writes of a chilling account of UFO possession that occurred behind the Iron Curtain.

"In the Soviet Union," Vallee reports, "not very long ago, an eminent scientist in the file of plasma research died under suspicious circumstances—he was murdered by a mentally disturbed woman who pushed him into the path of a train which was speeding into a Moscow subway station. The accused claimed that a 'voice' from space had instructed her to kill this particular man and she felt unable to resist the order."

Furthermore, the French scientist says, he has heard from "trustworthy sources" that Russian criminologists are disturbed about the recent increase in cases of this nature.

"Quite often," Vallee maintains, "mentally unstable people are known to run wildly across a street, protesting they are being pursued by Martians, but the present wave of mental troubles is an aspect of the UFO problem that deserves special attention."

We have long known that UFOs show no political preferences or respect for national boundaries. Aggressive acts have been committed worldwide by individuals who insist that they are in contact with extraterrestrials. Once contact has been established, they are doomed to do what is asked—whether they approve or not!

Here in the U.S., Brad Steiger, a respected former English professor turned author and parapsychologist, has been diligently gathering volumes of pertinent data. In the last few years, he has managed to amass an impressive collection of material dealing with the many peculiar side effects experienced by flying saucer eyewitnesses. He has gathered statistics on all sorts of "UFO oddities," including episodes involving instantaneous teleportation of observers; cases of enhanced psychic abilities; and information pertaining to the bane of all UFO researchers - the Men in Black. These areas all contain elements of the UFO possession syndrome.

A short time ago, Brad told me he had talked to a young serviceman who complained of hearing "beeps" inside his head. The loud and annoying noise began immediately after a UFO flew directly over him. Steiger was further convinced of the man's credibility because "as another researcher and I sat with the young man in a motel room, hundreds of miles away from my home, I heard him describe every room in my house and correctly identify objects within each room."

Another victim of UFO possession, a veteran of World War II, told Steiger how he was walking up a street in Italy one night shortly after the Allied occupation, when he heard a buzzing noise above him. The next thing he knew, he was in northern France. Not only had he traveled by some unknown means, but four months had elapsed of which he had no recall. As if to compensate for the loss of time, however, the soldier found he had suddenly developed clairvoyant abilities which he did not possess before the incident occurred.

"Today he lives in a large Midwestern city," Steiger said, "more disturbed than elated by his 'gift' from unknown donors."

In the July 1975 issue of *Probe the Unknown* magazine, Steiger talked about the morbid experience of a young married couple, Sam and Mary, who, in their spare time, had been attempting to track down and verify sightings of humanoid creatures made in their home state. They made it a regular policy to notify Brad of their findings.

One evening, after returning home from an interview with the witnesses of a humanoid sighting, Mary began feeling strange. A terrific headache sent her off to bed early. Once asleep, she was visited in her dreams by "grotesque entities" who told her that they wanted her and that she must leave her husband. They threatened violence if she did not obey. In subsequent "dreams," the confused woman saw "grim, dark-complexioned men beat Sam to death." Here, again, UFO researchers have noted many similar instances where space beings have shown they are able to manipulate the dreams of earthlings. Their "hold," once obtained, is enormous.

Mary's experience didn't end there, however, and the torment continued, becoming more oppressive with each day. Shortly afterwards, her telephone became—as Steiger so aptly phrased it—"an instrument of fear." Mary was awakened late one night, in the middle of one of her bizarre nightmares, by the ringing of the phone. Answering, she heard a cold, mechanical voice ask her, "Now are you ready to come over to our side?"

According to Steiger, Mary was later visited by a man who appeared at her front door, flashing impressive-looking telephone company credentials. He was anxious to know about her "problems." Sam later checked the man's papers and found his "impressive credentials" to be fake. The man didn't work for the phone company – in any capacity.

Immediately following the stranger's appearance, Mary began falling into deep, coma-like trances. These trances were usually prefaced "by a headache, a pain in the back of her neck, then a lapse of consciousness," and she seemed powerless to prevent their occurrence.

Needing assistance, the young couple contacted Steiger. He suggested they minimize the situation in their minds.

"The important thing is not to play their game," the author warned. "In many ways, their effect [that of the MIB] is like an echo. Cry out in fear, and they'll give you good reason to fear them."

They took Steiger's advice and were greatly relieved to find that the phenomena came to an abrupt halt.

ANOTHER CASE – UNDER THEIR SPELL

Sam and Mary were left in peace – but other individuals have not been set free so easily. Take the case of Hans Lauritzen. A trained engineer, Hans is not the type of person to be easily frightened or duped. Writing from his home in Copenhagen, Denmark, this reliable UFO witness filled me in on the details of his December 7, 1967, encounter with two disc-shaped craft.

"At the time, I was on a walking tour with four friends in a wooded area not far from Hareskoven. Because of a severe case of hepatitis, I found it difficult to keep up the brisk pace of my associates. I had to stop several times because I was so tired. At that time, my liver was extremely distended."

As the group passed a clearing, Lauritzen asked his friends if he might rest a few minutes. They, of course, said it was O.K.

"Suddenly, we all saw two great yellow globes about 50 yards from where we were standing. For some reason, at this point I asked if I could walk into the woods for ten minutes. My friends agreed. I had no intention of walking toward the UFOs, as we could not see them anymore. I seemed to be walking in a trance – like one who is being guided. I just walked. Then I felt the presence of something above but could not see anything."

At this point, Hans began to feel a throbbing pressure in his head, which seemed to bring on a telepathic conversation with whoever was "guiding" him.

"They told me I should give—and not receive. And that I should not be alone. And they said, 'You are only standing here by the help of your friends.' Then whoever was doing the talking seemed surprised and said, 'This is the first time.' I don't know exactly what he was referring to, except that he probably meant that it was the first time they had met anyone quite like myself. They told me that I had a very strong power and that it would soon become even stronger."

Hans asked the invisible voice "to make it so this power could not be misused." With this final request, the conversation ended. For some time afterwards, Hans continued to walk in a trance. Eventually, he found himself at the place where he had first seen the yellow globes.

"There was an open area which I decided to cross. I don't remember walking across it. All of a sudden, I heard my friends calling for me. I looked at my watch and saw that more than an hour had elapsed."

Returning to his friends, Hans was told that they had been searching for him during this period.

"They thought that I had gotten lost."

Strange things started to happen. Hans found himself running to their parked automobile. Only an hour before, he had barely been able to walk because of his liver condition.

"I realized that I had been cured of my otherwise chronic hepatitis. On my next visit to the clinic, the doctors told me that my liver had returned to its normal size. Blood tests showed that it was functioning as any healthy liver should!"

The medical experts could not offer any explanation for the change in Hans Lauritzen's physical condition.

"I didn't dare tell them about my contact," he admitted.

The oddest part of the story remains to be told. Soon after the experience, the Danish engineer found his entire life and personality beginning to change.

"I felt something spreading inside my body. Something was actually moving up along my spine from my lower back to the neck and to the back of my head. This movement was accompanied by a pleasurable feeling. It made me stand up and make strange movements and turns."

NEGATIVE PSYCHOLOGICAL EFFECTS

He explained that he was in a trance state much of the time.

"I just had to follow whoever was pulling my strings. Afterwards, I became extremely frightened as to what might be going on. I began to imagine all sorts of weird things!"

As it was, this "feeling" began to spread throughout his entire nervous system. After several months, pain would frequently shoot through his arms, chest, back and neck.

"I had never experienced such strong pains before in my life," Hans declared.

Gradually, however, the effects of the pain began to subside. Then Lauritzen found that he was frequently becoming overwhelmed by the most pleasurable states of mind.

"It was so wonderful," he said, "that it cannot be described."

On other occasions, the contactee said he felt a strong fear and anxiety, so much so that he was afraid to leave his apartment.

"I went through periods of extreme sorrow, depression and desperation. I have never experienced such severe mental suffering in all my life."

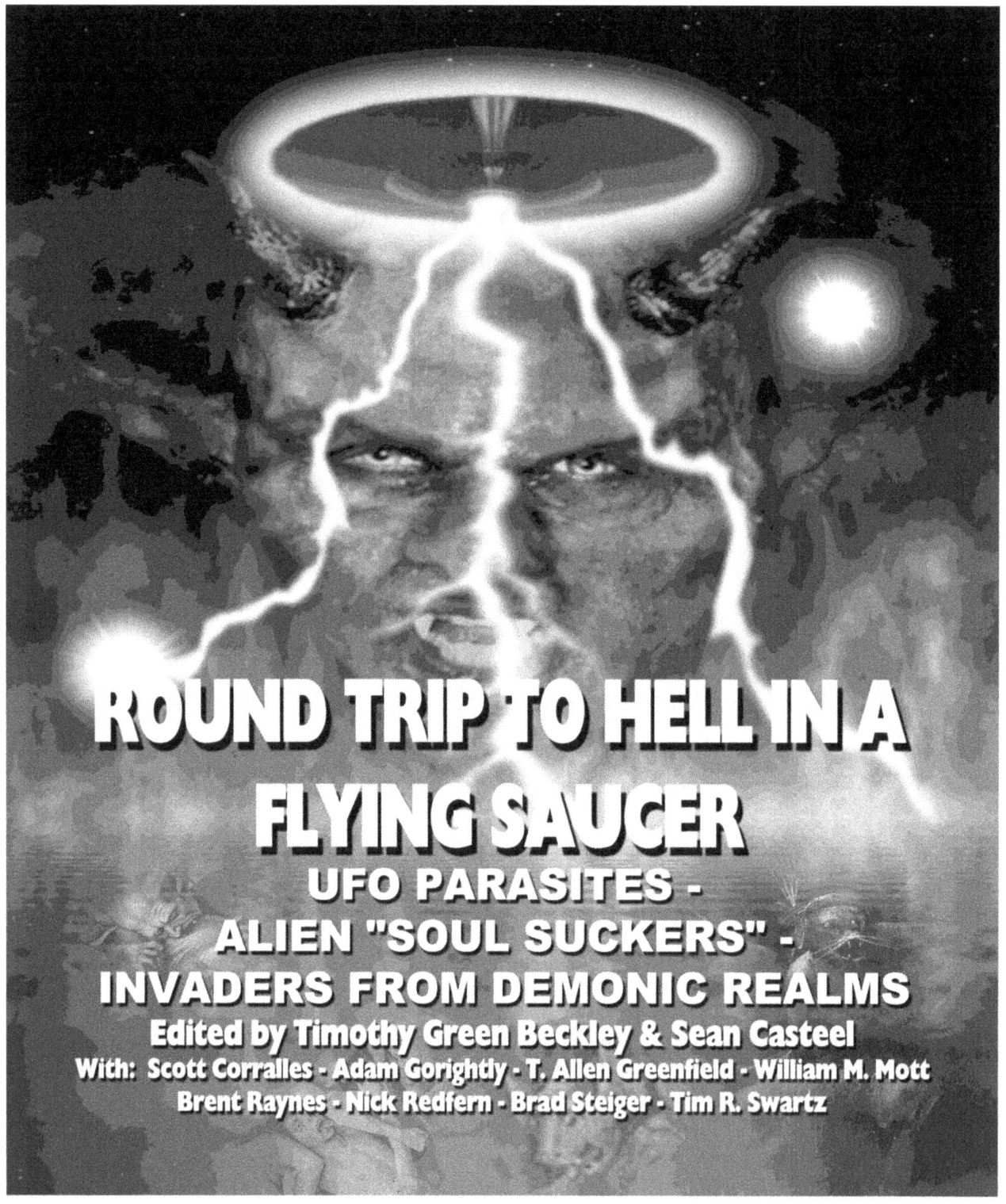

In our previously published book, *Round Trip To Hell In A Flying Saucer*, the authors relate how the UFO beings are often not so friendly to the citizens of planet Earth.

Over a century ago, Charles Fort let it be known that we were under the control and influence of some off-world power.

It was at this point that he began to realize he no longer had any free will to think and believe as he wished.

"I would converse with people, voicing opinions on a wide range of topics. Later, I discovered that whatever I had heard, I had to believe and act accordingly. Of course, this created great confusion. Strange thoughts started to come into focus. I knew they did not originate inside me because they were often of a very negative and destructive character. It was not possible for me to stop these thoughts or overpower them, although I tried. Believe me, I tried!"

Hans said that he had never before thought it possible that such a chaotic state of affairs could possibly exist in one person's mind! Eight years have passed and Hans finds himself once again leading a normal existence. When asked for his comments on the entire episode, he replied, "It has been the most wonderful and pleasurable experience of my entire life. On the other hand, it has also been the most painful, horrible thing that has ever happened to me. Before, I had a bad liver. Now, I am strong and healthy again. I am most thankful to the UFOs for having cured my chronic hepatitis, without which I would never have been able to resume my work and other normal activities."

Obviously both positive and negative factors have been experienced by those who have come within close range of these strange craft.

Realizing that something most peculiar is manifesting itself, we are still left with a gnawing question: is an invasion force poised at our atmospheric doorstep? And, if so, is their proposed takeover being done for our own welfare? Or for some as yet unknown – and perhaps sinister – reason?

Logically, we would like to believe that the metallic ships described eons ago by the pharaohs as "celestial sun discs" are manned by a super race of benevolent "space brothers" who harbor genuine concern for our world. But, then again, is this really the case? Are we actually being aided in our moment of need by "interplanetary wise men," or is some devious scheme unfolding as we ponder this very question?

Could it be that an interplanetary battle is being waged by rival starmen to gain control of Homo sapiens? Maybe, as some outspoken researchers have stated, a "war of the worlds" is being fought, not here on the physical plane but in some other dimension.

MASTERY OVER THE HUMAN RACE

Veteran investigators of the paranormal will undoubtedly recognize that attempts to gain mastery over the human race are nothing new. As intriguing as cases of UFO possession may be, a direct comparison can easily be found in the lore of the occult. Indeed, spirit and demonic possession have been written about for centuries. It is almost a commonplace phenomenon in theological and psychic circles. Only recently, because of the immense popularity of the motion picture "The Exorcist," has the subject come to the attention of the general public. Many moviegoers found this picture uncomfortably realistic.

Like the hideous demons of old, it would seem that at least some ufonauts have developed the ability to control certain individuals they have selected to do their bidding. Many times, I have sympathetically looked on—much like the young priest in "The Exorcist"—as a UFO observer undergoes a dramatic change in character and personality. It is uncanny – and difficult to rationally explain.

There is, however, another school of thought regarding this phenomenon.

Individuals such as Simon Swagger, whose story we detailed earlier, insist that any direct manipulation of humans by space people is being done for our benefit.

"I've been led to believe," Simon says, "that there is a grand event slated to occur in the not-too-distant future. I have no idea when this event will transpire, or what it will consist of, but I do know that it will be earthshaking and will affect almost everyone."

Another good example of what seems to be a "positive" case of UFO possession involves none other than Uri Geller, the extraordinary psychic. Reportedly, he is able to accomplish a variety of astonishing feats, including the bending of metal by means of psychokinesis; interfering with, and rendering inoperable, various electronic and mechanical devices; and beaming in on the telepathic thoughts of others. Geller has long been linked with extraterrestrials. He openly acknowledges that his powers originate from a source "outside" himself.

Dr. Andrija Puharich, the man responsible for bringing Uri to this country several years ago, admits that his gifted protégé is an agent for inhabitants of a certain zone. All the remarkable things that go on around Uri are, he says, directed by these "solar beings."

Though it has a definite Space Age twist, Uri's biography contains all the ingredients found in a suspenseful occult or gothic novel. During the occasions he slips into a hypnotic trance, Uri's features are said to change. In addition, a strange voice—definitely not his own—is heard from the psychic's mouth. Regaining consciousness, Uri has no recollection of what has transpired. And although Puharich has attempted to record these "foreign" tongues for posterity, he has constantly run into problems. When the tape is replayed, it is frequently blank. Other times, the cassette itself will vanish right out of the recorder.

Both Uri Geller and Simon Swagger are adamant that there is a specific reason why they have been selected to represent this unearthly power. They agree that some monumental event is slated to happen within a short time, and it's essential we be fully prepared for it.

Geller and Swagger also agree that the ufonauts are using them for the good of mankind. We are told that they have a definite plan and have simply decided to utilize human agents to get the job done faster.

Whatever the answers might be, an exhaustive study of the UFO puzzle shows "higher powers" are at play. They are attempting to systematically guide or influence our destiny. A sufficient number of strange occurrences have been reported which prove, beyond a reasonable doubt, that at least some of these "otherworldly travelers" are out to control the course of our civilization—if not by physical force, then by the direct manipulation of human minds!

PROJECT ALIEN MIND CONTROL -- UFO REVIEW SPECIAL

The dreaded Men in Black have taken their toll on witnessess. This first time ever close-up of a MIB was photographed by Tim Beckley across the street from UFO researcher John J. Robinson, Jersey City, NJ.

ALIEN ABDUCTION AND MIND CONTROL: ARE MERE MORTALS TO BLAME?

By Sean Casteel

"Among ufologists," Martin Cannon writes, "the term 'abduction' has come to refer to an infinitely confounding experience, or matrix of experiences, shared by a dizzying number of individuals, who claim that travelers from the stars have scooped them out of their beds, or snatched them from their cars, and subjected them to interrogations, quasi-medical examinations, and 'instruction' periods."

PROJECT ALIEN MIND CONTROL -- UFO REVIEW SPECIAL

THERE are a few alternative explanations for the alien abduction phenomenon, the most prevalent being that the experience does not involve actual aliens at all but is instead a complex, human-driven tool used for purposes of mind control. It is said that the alien abduction phenomenon is actually a cover story intended to conceal something even more disturbing than aliens, that being an encroachment on the very souls of those chosen to be victims of government and military experiments that seek to control the workings of the human brain itself for purposes of psychological warfare and for intelligence operations requiring a "zombie" type agent who has no idea he is carrying out a covert mission.

This idea is not exactly new. It entered into the pop culture zeitgeist as early as the 1962 thriller film "The Manchurian Candidate," in which a team of American soldiers taken prisoner during the Korean War are brainwashed by their Chinese captors into various heinous acts, with one in particular charged to assassinate a candidate for president. The assassin is merely responding to post-hypnotic suggestion as he goes through the motions of his role in some dark political intrigue indeed.

But a lot has happened since, and Timothy Green Beckley of Global Communications has released a slew of books that deal with the subject from a decidedly 21st century perspective, including the fascinating overlap between mind control technology and alien abduction.

For example, there is the Global Communications book, ***Nightmare Alley: Fearsome Tales Of Alien Abduction***, which begins with capsule histories of some of the better-known abduction cases, such as the 1961 Betty and Barney Hill encounter that became a kind of template for the thousands of cases that came later. The cases in the book were compiled by Beckley, his editorial and art consultant, William Kern, and B.J. Booth, a researcher known for his website www.ufocasebook.com. The team has gathered cases that stretch from the Hills to Betty Andreasson Luca on to the 2004 Francis Family abduction and the Clayton and Donna Lee event of 2005. As an easily digestible overview of the abduction phenomenon, it has few peers in the field.

But in the later sections of the book, the alien factor is moved to a backburner and the all-too-human quest for control of the individual's mind is given an excellent scholarly and detailed treatment by researcher and writer Martin Cannon. Cannon begins by attempting to shine a light on what alien abduction is said to be.

"Among ufologists," Cannon writes, "the term 'abduction' has come to refer to an infinitely confounding experience, or matrix of experiences, shared by a dizzying number of individuals, who claim that travelers from the stars have scooped them out of their beds, or snatched them from their cars, and subjected them to interrogations, quasi-medical examinations, and 'instruction' periods."

He goes on to say that these sessions are said to occur within alien spacecraft and include terrifying details "reminiscent of the tortures inflicted in Germany's death camps."

The abductees often, though not always, lose all memory of these events and find themselves back in their beds or cars unable to account for "missing time." Hypnosis or some other trigger can bring back these "haunted hours" in an explosion of recollection, and the abductee often begins to recall a history of similar experiences stretching all the way back to childhood. Cannon also expresses amazement that abductees, in spite of their vividly-recalled agonies, claim to "love" their alien tormentors.

Cannon quickly shifts gears and begins to offer his own theories about the abduction phenomenon.

"I posit that the abductees have been abducted," he writes. "Yet they are also spewing fantasy – or, more precisely, they have been given a set of lies to repeat and believe. If my hypothesis proves true, then we must accept the following: The kidnapping is real. The fear is real. The pain is real. The instruction is real. But the little grey men from Zeti Reticuli are not real; they are constructs, Halloween masks meant to disguise the real faces of the controllers. The abductors may not be visitors from Beyond; rather, they may be a symptom of the carcinoma which blackens our body politic. The fault lies not in our stars, but in ourselves."

There is substantial evidence, according to Cannon, that links members of this country's intelligence community, to include the CIA, the Defense Advanced Research Projects Agency and the Office of Naval Intelligence, with "the esoteric technology of mind control."

"For decades," Cannon continues, "'spy-chiatrists' working mostly behind the scenes – on college campuses, in CIA-sponsored institutes, and (most heinously) in prisons – have experimented with erasure of memory, hypnotic resistance to torture, truth serums, post-hypnotic suggestion, rapid induction of hypnosis, electronic stimulation of the brain, non-iodizing radiation, microwave induction of intra-cerebral 'voices,' and a host of even more disturbing technologies. Some of the projects exploring these areas were ARTICHOKE, BLUEBIRD, PANDORA, MK-DELTA, MK-SEARCH and the infamous MK-ULTRA."

Cannon said his research includes reading nearly every available book on the subject, as well as all the relevant congressional testimony, plus spending much time in university libraries reading relevant articles. He also conducted numerous interviews and was allowed to see the files of John Marks, the author of ***The Search For 'The Manchurian Candidate***, which included some 20,000 pages of CIA and Defense Department documents, interviews, scientific articles, letters, etc.

Cannon has certainly done his homework, which leads him to conclude that striking advances have been made in the field of brainwashing despite false and perjured claims made before Congress that these efforts had met with little success and had been discontinued. He also restates his belief that UFO abduction may be a continuation of clandestine mind control operations.

The next section of Cannon's report is a fascinating overview of the known technology so far and introduces the reader to the term "wavies," or people who claim to be victims of clandestine bombardment with non-ionizing radiation, or microwaves.

"They report sudden changes in psychological states, alteration of sleep patterns, intra-cerebral voices and other sounds, and physiological effects. Are these troubled individuals seeking an exterior rationale for their mental problems? Maybe. Indeed, I'm sure that such is the case in many instances. But the fact is that the literature on the behavioral effects of microwaves, extra-low-frequencies and ultra-sonics is such that we cannot blithely dismiss all such claims."

When did this research really begin? Cannon says that in the early years of the 20th century, Nikola Tesla seems to have stumbled upon certain of the behavioral effects of electromagnetic exposure, and Cannon also cites a report from the 1930s in which two scientists claimed to be able to electrically stimulate the human nervous system by remote control. Meanwhile, who knows what has been achieved over the last few decades or what is the current state-of-the-art in mind control technology?

Cannon returns to his basic thesis, writing, "The abduction enigma contains within it sub-mysteries that slide into the mind control scenario with surprising ease, even elegance. As we have seen, the MK-ULTRA thesis explains the reports of abductee intra-cerebral implants (particularly reports involving nosebleeds), unusual scars, 'telepathic' communication (i.e., externally induced intra-cerebral voices) concurrent with or following the abduction, allegations that some abductees hear unusual sound effects, haywire electronic devices in abductee homes, personality shifts, 'training films,' manipulation of religious imagery, and missing time. Needless to say, the thesis of clandestine government experimentation readily accounts for abductee claims of human beings 'working' with the aliens and for the government harassment that plays so prominent a role in certain abductee reports."

Another release from Global Communications, *Mind Stalkers: Mind Control of the Masses*, covers some similar ground. The authors, Commander X and Tim R. Swartz, also offer some interesting history of what is known about mind control technology as well as some scientific background on how the various devices actually work. Chapters on secret experiments with drugs, subliminal seduction, electronics, microwaves, implants and "mind machines" in general are stuffed with frightening information on the potential enslavement of the human mind to those who can covertly manipulate it. The drive to create a "super soldier" quickly devolves into the search for an iron grip on mass consciousness that has been sought by every totalitarian leader throughout human history, only now such a nightmarish possibility may be terrifyingly within reach with the mere flick of an "on switch."

Swartz and Commander X also tackle the thorny subject of human mind control as the true origin of UFO abduction.

"UFO literature is filled with hundreds of cases," the two authors write, "in which observers have been subjected to continuous harassments following an encounter with a UFO. Some witnesses report strange, ghost-like phenomena in their homes. In other cases, weird, mechanical-sounding voices, purported to be 'messages' from extraterrestrials, begin emanating from their phones, radios and televisions."

The authors point out that scant research has been done into this view of the phenomenon, and investigators are loathe to touch the subject, believing that the witnesses who complain of such harassment are most likely mentally ill. It is a kind of Catch-22 that victims must suffer through: after a prolonged period of skilled mismanagement of their brains, they are hardly credible witnesses who can coherently PROVE their stories. But the authors say that cases of UFO mind control are almost always identical.

"The eyewitness goes through a period of anxiety," the authors explain, "during which he is unable to consciously remember certain aspects of the incident. Within months, the personality of the observer actually changes. Eventually, it may change to the point where he finds it impossible to get along with coworkers, friends or even family. Personal tragedy seems to strike many of those who have had UFO experiences."

The person may also develop certain "gifts" or abilities, such as powers of ESP, precognition or psycho-kinesis, as well as a heightened intelligence level or an unusual increase in physical strength. These abilities may manifest themselves shortly before a person is about to be controlled. Soon he may begin slipping into a kind of trance, and it will appear an alien intelligence has taken over his body and is using his brain.

But nevertheless, we could still be dealing with human "controllers," the authors insist, as they cite the research of Dr. Helmut Lammer, who recounts the stories of how some UFO abductees have been kidnapped by military personnel and taken to hospitals and/or military facilities which are often described as being underground.

"Especially disconcerting is the fact that abductees recall seeing military intelligence personnel together with alien beings," Commander X and Swartz write, "working side by side in these secret facilities. Researchers in the field of mind control suggest that these cases are evidence that the whole UFO abduction phenomenon is staged by the intelligence community as a cover for their illegal experiments."

The authors go on to say that Lammer's research suggests that abductees are often harassed by dark, unmarked helicopters that fly around their houses. The mysterious helicopter activity goes back to the late 1960s and early 1970s, when they showed an apparent interest in animal mutilations, but not, at the time, in alleged UFO abductees. Still, UFO researcher Raymond Fowler reported some helicopter activity in connection with UFO witnesses during the 1970s, so the phenomenon is not without an earlier precedent.

Meanwhile, the idea that the black helicopters are sent to "spy" on UFO witnesses is called absurd by Martin Cannon, who says if the military were seeking information on abductees they would certainly go about it in a much more subtle manner. The late abduction researcher Budd Hopkins once similarly stated that if the intelligence community wanted to spy on abductees, they could probably stand two blocks away and point a cufflink at their intended targets, so far advanced was their espionage technology. In any case, the true mission of the black helicopters remains unknown.

Abductee Debbie Jordan reported in her book *Abducted!* that she was kidnapped, drugged and taken to a kind of military hospital where she was examined by a medical doctor. This doctor told her he was going to remove a "bug" from her ear and proceeded to take out an implant that resembled a BB. Also, some of author Katharina Wilson's experiences are reminiscent of reported mind control experiments. She writes of a flashback from her childhood in which she remembers being forced into what appeared to be a Skinner Box that may have been used for behavior modification purposes. In some military abduction cases military doctors searched for implants and sometimes even implanted the abductee with what may have been a manmade implant.

Mind Stalkers also includes an "Index Of Secret Mind Control Projects" that provides a quick rundown of the often confusing military codenames and the "alphabet soup" by which some of the various programs came to be called.

It is an interesting irony that what makes the whole complex of the abduction mystery so sinister and shocking is not the presence of aliens from another planet but the dark machinations of a completely human enemy of mankind – perhaps our own government and military.

Many UFO abductees report that they and their families are often harassed by black, unmarked helicopters that repeatedly fly around their houses at all hours of the day and night.

In 2010, Jon Meyers of St. Louis, Missouri, said that while he was jogging in a local park, several disc-shaped craft suddenly appeared and took up position directly above him. The UFO closest to him shot out a "sparkling beam of bright light" which enveloped and paralyzed him. While he was frozen in place, Meyers said that his head was filled with "voices" telling him that he had a mission to accomplish at a future date in order to convince the people of Earth about the reality of extraterrestrials.

SHADOW UNIVERSE OF ALIEN THOUGHT CONTROL

Are the aliens offering solutions to mankind's problems as a kind of Trojan horse in order to get their foot in the door so they can lead us to a totalitarian form of world government?

By Sean Casteel

PROJECT ALIEN MIND CONTROL -- UFO REVIEW SPECIAL

IN the New Millennium, as in decades past, the appearance of UFOs and their shadowy crew members may in fact be a political tool being used to reshape the patterns of our collective thought processes to the aliens' advantage, which forces us to ask questions like:

*** Are the extraterrestrials here implementing plans to take control of the planet?

*** Are the aliens offering solutions to mankind's problems as a kind of Trojan horse in order to get their foot in the door so they can lead us to a totalitarian form of world government?

*** Do the extraterrestrials (or ultra-terrestrials, as they are sometimes called) utilize religion – and fundamentalism in particular – to influence and even control the current program of terrorism?

*** Will mankind one day be ruled over by hybrid human/aliens who superior mental powers will completely subjugate us?

*** Have we secretly achieved a new military technology that may one day provide us with effective weapons to use against an alien invasion?

*** And finally, have the extraterrestrials found an ally in high-profile UFO researcher and advocate Dr. Steven Greer and his at one time popular Disclosure Project organization?

According to journalist and author Michael Brownlee, the answer to all of those questions is a resounding yes!

Brownlee published a two-part essay on what he sees as the potential peril certain UFO researchers such as Dr. Steven Greer may be placing our civilization in – either knowingly or unknowingly – by helping to popularize the unproven notion that the extraterrestrials are here to be helpful, benevolent friends of mankind. (Dr. Greer declined to be interviewed for this chapter, citing his busy schedule.)

A TARNISHED HERO

Brownlee initially viewed Greer as a hero.

"In 1997," Brownlee said, "which was a pivotal year in this field, I went to a conference in Phoenix, Arizona. It was a Prophets Conference, and one of the speakers there was Steven Greer. I'd heard of Steven. I had been reading some of his material and was very interested because he was the only one who, at least in the title of his organization [which is the Center for the Study of Extraterrestrial Intelligence], was talking about studying the extraterrestrials themselves. I thought his efforts toward disclosing the presence of extraterrestrials were very courageous and heroic.

"And I know he was suffering a lot of persecution at that time," Brownlee continued. "The person who was closest to him in that work died of cancer. Dr. Greer also suffered from cancer, and they felt very strongly that the cancers were implanted by someone who wanted to stop them. I was just very touched. I thought he was very compassionate, brilliant man, passionate and doing something worthwhile."

But since then Brownlee says his opinion has changed.

"Whether for him it's knowingly or unknowingly," Brownlee said, "it would appear that Dr. Greer has been essentially 'co-opted' by the extraterrestrials who are visiting the Earth at this time."

In other words, the aliens have taken control of Greer, at least in terms of what he says publicly. Meanwhile, Brownlee credits a reclusive spiritual leader named Marshall Summers with helping him to gain what he now feels is a more accurate viewpoint on both Greer and what the aliens really want.

A WARNING FROM HUMANITY'S ALLIES

"At a UFO Expo in California," Brownlee said, "I ran into people who had an underground version of a book that I had not heard of. It was called *The Allies of Humanity*, written by this man named Marshall Summers. The book's had a galvanizing effect on my life, certainly, and it has on a lot of other people as well, because the perspective that it presents is just totally unprecedented in this field. It's not research. It's not about the phenomenon per se. It is a look at what's happening."

The "Allies" of the book's title are a group of friendly extraterrestrials who are sending a warning to mankind about the coming colonization of the Earth by less benevolent aliens intent on manipulating mankind into an ultimate submission.

"This book contains information," Brownlee said, "that just unravels the whole mystery of the extraterrestrial activities and presence on this planet. And I say that not based upon something I just want to believe, because there's a lot of material in it that's damned uncomfortable."

Our prior attempts to understand the situation, Brownlee says, have been woefully inadequate.

"The biggest problem we've had in the UFO/ET research community," he said, "is that this whole business of UFOs and extraterrestrials has been thoroughly enigmatic. It has just been a mystery. We haven't been able to penetrate it no matter how much research we do. After more than sixty years of hammering away at it, we haven't gotten much closer than we were in 1947. We have a lot of different ideas and theories and experiences, and they're all conflicting."

But Summers' book, while it is helpful to Brownlee in terms of getting a handle on the phenomenon, hasn't been welcomed with open arms by the UFO community.

"One of the things I've noticed," Brownlee said, "is that the material presented in this little book is highly unpopular in the UFO community. Because it presents a viewpoint that a lot of people would just not like to be true. The aliens are, just like [well-known UFO researcher] David Jacobs says, implementing plans to take control of this planet.

"Not to destroy humanity," he continued, "but to take control. And Steven Greer has become their most effective ally and ambassador with the human race. He's gone from responding to a deep passion within him to being used by the extraterrestrials. And as I say, I don't know whether he's aware of it or not. But, unfortunately, that's the position he seems to be in. So in my eyes he's gone from being a hero for being so courageous to being a very, very dangerous force in the world today."

The Allies of Humanity, written by Marshall Summers, was very influential for Brownlee. The "Allies" of the book's title are a group of friendly extraterrestrials who are sending a warning to mankind about the coming colonization of the Earth by less benevolent aliens intent on manipulating mankind into an ultimate submission.

PROJECT ALIEN MIND CONTROL -- UFO REVIEW SPECIAL

A QUESTION OF WHAT IS MANMADE AND WHAT IS NOT

Brownlee vigorously contests certain opinions expressed by Greer, including Greer's claim that the majority of UFOs sighted are really manmade devices.

"Of course," Brownlee said, "the literature is filled with stories of how we have captured craft or downed spacecraft, and we have been working very hard to reverse-engineer them at Area 51 and other places. We've been hearing all that for years. And Greer was talking about that in his early years. But he started saying that, 'Well, what's really going on is that most of the UFOs in the sky are manmade.'

"Now, there is absolutely no evidence for that. It is an assertion on his part that is not backed up by evidence. He said, 'And we can prove it,' again and again. But he doesn't offer any proof. He doesn't offer any documentation whatsoever I have no doubt that the government has been doing its best to reverse-engineer alien craft technology, but it's a long way from that to saying that the majority of UFOs are manmade."

Brownlee also disputes Greer's claim that the abduction phenomenon is also a human effort.

"This is called 'Escalation of Rhetoric,'" Brownlee explained. "Years ago, and I have heard Greer talk about this, he was saying that, based upon the work of Helmut Lammer, who wrote about MILAB abductions, Greer said it looks like we're in the business of doing abductions. It's absolutely true that Helmut Lammer wrote about military-based abductions, human-based abductions. He says he doesn't know why it's happening. He just said it appears to be happening, but he also makes crystal clear that, based upon his research, this amounts to a very small fraction of the abductions that are taking place.

"So Greer started using Helmut's research on MILAB abductions," Brownlee went on, "and he escalated the rhetoric to start saying that all abductions are perpetrated by humans. All of them. Now, again, there is absolutely no evidence to that effect. There is no way he could even know that. If you look at the evidence, if you look at the studies that have been done, if you look at all the abduction research, on balance you'd have to say that is a completely ludicrous claim. Why is he making it? It's very odd. It's even odder that no one calls him on it."

But what if Dr. Greer is right, at least partially? How would a "hoaxed abduction," the kind put forth by Greer, typically play itself out?

"My understanding is," Brownlee replied, "that it follows much the same course. The one difference sometimes is that the abductees are taken to underground facility. An underground, apparently MILITARY facility where they see lots of armed soldiers and things like that.

"Now, if you ask David Jacobs about this, he will say, well, it's pretty obvious now. We know from research on hundreds and hundreds if not thousands of abductees that human-appearing beings often show up in abduction scenarios. And what he proposes is that those are not humans at all but are in fact hybrids. The hybrids are increasingly responsible for the abduction program. So to assert that they are human is a wild assertion, devoid of evidence."

However, in spite of what Brownlee considers to be Greer's false claims, Greer still provides an accurate barometer of what the aliens really want, says Brownlee.

"What I have learned about Steven Greer," Brownlee said, "is if you want to know what the extraterrestrials are concerned about, what they're worried about, what they're up to, pay attention to what Dr. Greer is saying and doing. He can give us the best insight into their strategy of almost anybody on the planet. But you have to look at it from the perspective that what's going on here is essentially a clandestine takeover of the planet. And, again, this is not about destroying humanity or destroying the planet. That's ludicrous. They want CONTROL. It's just that simple."

TAKING CONTROL THROUGH GUILT

One method the aliens are using to manipulate our thinking is the time-honored ploy of making humanity feel guilty.

"The really stark thing that comes through everything else," Brownlee said, "is the statement that humans are the real problem in the universe. That's an outrageous statement. It is based upon a species-wide guilt, if you will. It's like, 'Oh, man, we're really bad. We're really screwed up.' And that's exactly where we're most vulnerable. So the extraterrestrials come and abduct our people and they tell them – and you can read the reports from [Harvard psychiatrist Dr. John]

Mack or Jacobs or [seminal abduction researcher] Budd Hopkins. It doesn't matter. It's all the same. The point the extraterrestrials make is 'You guys are screwing up your planet.'

"Well, they don't say it this way, but the feeling is, 'You're bad. You're screwed up. You need us to come and straighten things out.' From a psychological perspective, that is the basis of a codependent relationship. That's exactly what they're trying to create. They want us dependent on them. They want us controlled. We're useful to them because their numbers aren't very large. They've got a lot of work to do here and they need our labor."

One primary motivation for the alien takeover may be simple, old-fashioned greed.

"The world holds incredible resources that are pretty rare in the universe," Brownlee theorizes. "Those resources include biological resources, they include mineral resources and perhaps some other things. They don't want us, for instance, destroying our ecological system because it's bad business for them. It screws up their plans."

The aliens offer solutions to mankind's problems as a kind of Trojan horse in order to get their foot in the door so they can lead us to a totalitarian form of government.

"The message of fascism," Brownlee said, "is always 'This will solve all problems.' What we're looking at are the signs of a fascist takeover that, if it is not exposed and resisted, will wind up being not just a fascist state but a fascist world.

ALIENS IN THE MENTAL REALM

"It's not like the aliens are going to come down as aliens and run things. No, they don't function that way. The Allies [the informants in Marshall Summers' aforementioned book] present a very interesting idea. And that is that the aliens are breeding hybrids to be the new rulers, the new leaders, of this world. They will look like humans, only they will be very, very powerful, particularly in what the Allies refer to as the 'mental environment.'

"The particular aliens that are here now, while they're technologically advanced, they don't have great legions, they don't have great military forces. That's not how they work. You can only take physical technology to a certain point in the evolution of life in the universe. What's beyond physical technology is the technology of the mental realm. And that's where they excel."

Brownlee made reference to Harvard abduction researcher, the late Dr. John Mack, to drive his point home.

"Even John Mack," Brownlee said, "who took a fairly positive view towards the alien presence here, he said the most common form of contact between humans and extraterrestrials is in the dream state. In other words, they can enter our dreams. They can plant images, ideas, emotions, thoughts, impulses. They're very good at that. And we're just so wide open that we don't even know it's going on, for the most part.

"In the mental realm," he continued, "they are very effective and we are unfortunately very naïve. So one of the ways that this plays out is in one of the key areas of alien activity—the manipulation of our religious and spiritual beliefs. They are very aware of our lack of sophistication and they are able to easily manipulate people who are particularly prone to fanatical belief, fundamentalism, in all of its varieties around the world. They can be very influential."

This has frightening implications on a global scale, according to Brownlee.

"One of the astonishing things that we ultimately learn out of this," he said, "is the extent to which the extraterrestrials are operating behind the scenes in world affairs today, influencing key people. And one of the great problems that we have in the world today, that's pushed us to the brink of global warfare, is this explosion of Islamic fundamentalism."

Brownlee again cited the Allies of Humanity as his source for this belief.

"The suggestion is that the extraterrestrials are meeting some resistance in the Western World," he said. "Meaning that we aren't just falling over for their program here. So they have decided to stir up some reprisals and to extract a little pain. Those are the roots, if you will, of the September 11 attack and the whole terrorist effort that has been building and escalating and has pushed us literally to war. Now, I think that's a pretty extraordinary hypothesis, and if there's any basis to it at all, it's something we should be looking at. I mean, talk about a conspiracy theory! That's about as big as it gets."

ANOTHER UNDECLARED WAR

On top of that, the aliens have begun another form of warfare.

"Craft have flown over military bases with nuclear missiles," Brownlee said, "and shut them down. They just shut the missiles down. People couldn't even restart them. There is no way that that could not be interpreted as a blatantly hostile act. If we did anything like that, to any other country, what would happen? It would be instant cause for war, right?

"It's a pretty universal principle. You enter my territory and you brandish weapons – or not even weapons, but just give a show of force, a show of power – that's throwing down the gauntlet. I mean, you've violated my territory, damn it! And what's interesting is our response to that. Our military forces, when events like that have happened, have found themselves to be completely powerless. There was nothing that they could do.

"Do you want the world to know that you were humiliated by someone like that? Absolutely not. You don't even have to talk about overflights. As Jacobs and others have done, you could simply talk about the abductions that are going on. They are a flagrant and fundamental violation of human rights and freedoms. You can't interpret it any other way. That's hostile.

"So the rhetorical claim that Steven Greer makes, that the aliens have no hostile intentions whatsoever, is preposterous. Again, it is an illogical, undocumented, unproven claim. Why is he making this claim? On whose behalf is he making such a claim?"

The aliens are also concerned that humanity may one day be able to defend itself militarily against an alien invasion.

"I know of people," Brownlee said, "who are involved in space defense projects and who are very consciously aware that what they're doing is developing systems to defend against the extraterrestrials. It's happening. It's not just pie-in-the-sky or a rumor; it's actually happening. They're working on it.

"There are pretty good indications," he continued, "that the whole Star Wars missile defense effort has very little to do with terrorism and rogue states on this planet. I think it's much more likely that those systems are early attempts to design systems to build a shield against extraterrestrial incursion. I know it's not a politically popular viewpoint, but I think it's worth considering. And if that were true, it would kind of explain the way that some of those programs have been handled, the secrecy around them, the kind of skittishness that our government has had about them."

DO ALIENS CONTROL THE OVERALL CONSPIRACY?

In spite of those possibly heroic machinations behind the scenes, there is still the REAL conspiracy to be dealt with, as Brownlee sees it.

"We talk about this dark conspiracy," he said, "of the wealthy and so on. It's not difficult to imagine that those people in positions of power are again either knowingly or unknowingly co-opted by the extraterrestrials. Yeah, there's a conspiracy, all right, but it's much larger than our conspiracy theorists have been talking about. We've been talking about human conspiracies here. Well, all human conspiracies are being manipulated by the extraterrestrials, essentially.

"We need to start understanding what they're up to. We need to start seeing the patterns of manipulation. We need to start seeing their strategies and their programs. We need to know what this hybridization program is about. We need to understand why they're manipulating religious and political and economic leaders throughout the world. We need to understand why they're acclimating us to their presence in every possible way they can, through the media, through entertainment, a variety of ways. They're getting us comfortable with the idea that aliens are among us."

All of which paints a dark picture, indeed. But there is more.

"We are on the brink of losing our freedom," Brownlee cautioned, "of losing our sovereignty, and we're not aware of it. And we need to become aware. We need to help other people become aware. And that's a very big challenge."

ABOUT MICHAEL BROWNLEE

Michael Brownlee is an author, publisher and journalist reporting on the "transformation of consciousness now unfolding on the planet." He cofounded Visibility Unlimited, LLC, a publishing venture committed to "communication that creates," and edited and published "Awakening World," an online magazine. Brownlee has conducted workshops on "Understanding the Extraterrestrial Presence in the World Today," an introduction to the mystery of "contact" and the growing challenge to our human freedom as well as other programs that provide an "introduction to the new paradigm of consciousness that is rapidly reshaping our world."

ABOUT STEVEN GREER, M.D.

Steven M. Greer, M.D., is the founder of The Disclosure Project, The Center for the Study of Extraterrestrial Intelligence (CSETI) and The Orion Project.

He presided over the National Press Club Disclosure Event in May, 2001. Over 20 military, government, intelligence and corporate witnesses presented compelling testimony regarding the existence of extraterrestrial life forms visiting the planet and the reverse-engineering of the energy and propulsion systems of their craft.

A lifetime member of Alpha Omega Alpha, the nation's most prestigious medical honor society, Dr. Greer has now retired as an emergency physician to work full time on the various issues that accompany the UFO phenomenon. During part of his career, he was chairman of the Department of Emergency Medicine at Caldwell Memorial Hospital in North Carolina.

He is the author of four books and multiple DVDs on the UFO/ET subject. He teaches groups throughout the world how to make peaceful contact with extraterrestrial civilizations and continues to research bringing truly alternative energy sources out to the public. Dr. Greer has been seen and heard by millions worldwide on CBS, the BBC, The Discovery Channel, The History Channel and through many other news sources.

PROJECT ALIEN MIND CONTROL -- UFO REVIEW SPECIAL

NOT long after my own encounter with strange aerial phenomena, I began to see a link between UFOs to such seemingly disparate topics as psychedelics, psychotronics and ritual magick. As the years pass, the Extraterrestrial Hypothesis (ETH) makes far less sense to this observer than other theories, ranging from mind control conspiracies, or – on the other hand – fissures in the space/time continuum which provide a portal of entry for ghostly apparitions that can be saucer-shaped or even take on the form of Moth-Men, Chupacabras or the Blessed Virgin Mary.

UFOs encompass a wide range of phenomena and cannot be categorized simply in terms of little grey-skinned buggers from Zeta-Reticuli shoving probes up human rectums. (Ouch!) To me, the term "UFO" simply suggests something unexplainable hovering in outer or inner space, whether it is machine-like elves encountered under the influence of DMT, or nuts-and-bolts craft performing inexplicable aerial maneuvers over Area 51.

UFOs are limited only by our imaginations, and to consider them merely craft from another galaxy is as narrow a view as postulating that newborn babes are delivered exclusively by storks. UFO's are also, in my estimation, a product of altered consciousness, which is not to suggest that all sightings are in part, or in whole, complete confabulations. What I'm suggesting is that in order to observe UFOs, one must often enter into a more receptive state, much like a psychic or channeler tuning into voices or subtle energies. Channelers must first induce in themselves a trance state before being able to contact "voices from the beyond." The same goes for magical workings wherein magicians carry out rituals in order to invoke spirits and/or demons.

A corollary to the above statement is the famed Amalantrah Working of legendary occultist Aleister Crowley, which consisted of a series of visions he received from January through March of 1918 via his then "Scarlet Woman," Roddie Minor. Throughout his life, Crowley had a number of Scarlet Women who acted as "Channels" for otherworldly transmissions of angelic and/or demonic origin. The Scarlet Woman also played a large part in Crowley's notorious sex rituals, at times combining drugs and bestiality to stir up those strange energies into which good ol' Uncle Al was trying to tap. To quote Crowley chronicler Kenneth Grant from *Aleister **Crowley and the Hidden God***:

Crowley was aware of the possibility of opening the spatial gateways and of admitting an extraterrestrial Current in the human life-wave...It is an occult tradition – and Lovecraft gave it persistent utterance in his writings – that some transfinite and superhuman power is marshaling its forces with intent to invade and take possession of this planet... This is reminiscent of Charles Fort's dark hints about a secret society on earth already in contact with cosmic beings and, perhaps, preparing the way for their advent. Crowley dispels the aura of evil with which these authors (Lovecraft and Fort) invest the fact; he prefers to interpret it Thelemically, not as an attack upon human consciousness by an extra-terrestrial and alien entity but as an expansion of consciousness from within, to embrace other stars and to absorb their energies into a system that is thereby enriched and rendered truly cosmic by the process.

It was through the Amalantrah Working – which included the ingestion of hashish and mescaline in its rituals – that Crowley came into contact with an interdimensional entity named Lam, who by the way just happens to be a dead ringer for the popular conception of the "Grey" alien depicted on the cover of Whitley Strieber's **Communion**. Crowley called them "Enochian entities" because he purportedly contacted them by using "Enochian calls," a Cabalistic system/language devised by the 17th century Elizabethan magician, Dr. John Dee. From this alleged encounter, some have inferred that the industrious Mr. Crowley intentionally opened a portal of entry through the practice of ritual magick, which allowed the likes of Lam and other "alien greys" a passageway onto the Earth plane. Dr. John Dee and his "scryer," Edward Kelly, had their own strange encounters with – as they called them – "little men" who moved about "in a little fiery cloud." Thus a pattern exists in the lore of ritual magic connecting UFOs to sorcery.

Some now believe that what Crowley tapped into was the same cosmic current that helped launch the current rash of alien abductions, as reported by such UFO researchers as Budd Hopkins, John Mack, David Jacobs, et al. When making these connections, bear in mind that many abductees recall their encounters with these grey-skinned creatures only after they've been hypnotically regressed. Once again, we see that trance states – not unlike those altered states of consciousness produced during rituals such as the Amalantrah

Working – are often the triggering factor which opens up a portal for these strange entities. According to Kenneth Grant, this tradition has been continued by current day adepts of Crowley, who follow in his footsteps practicing ritual magic to invoke these "alien entities."

In *Outside the Circles of Time*, Grant writes:

"Some believe that the UFO phenomena are part of the "miracle," and a mounting mass of evidence seems to suggest that mysterious entities have been located within the earth's ambience for countless centuries and that more and more people are being born with an innate ability to see, or in some way sense, their presence....Prayer for deific intervention in ancient times has now became a *"cri de Coeur"* to extraterrestrial or interdimensional entities, according to whether the manifestations are viewed as occurring within man's consciousness, or outside himself in apparently objective but often-invisible entities. New Isis Lodge has in its archives the sigils of some of these entities. The sigils come from a grimoire of unknown origin which forms part of the dark quabalahs of Besqul, located by magicians in the Tunnel of Quliefi. The grimoire describes Four Gates of extraterrestrial entry into, and emergence from, the known Universe."

What Grant is speaking of is a form of ritual magick practiced by such groups as the Golden Dawn and the Ordo Templi Orientis (O.T.O.). "Sigils" are line drawings and diagrams that serve as signatures of entities accessible to a trained magician familiar with "Enochian calls" and other methods of summoning "spirits." A grimoire is a directory of such sigils and a manual for their use.

A noted disciple of Crowley's, Jack Parsons – one time head of the California branch of the O.T.O., and renowned rocket scientist – carried on this tradition of interdimensional contact when, in 1946 – with the aid of "Frater H." – he made contact with some sort of entities not at all unlike Crowley's "Lam." This all took place during a series of magic rituals deemed The Babalon Workings. What makes this story all the more bizarre is that Parsons' accomplice in this endeavor – the aforementioned Frater H. – became more commonly known afterwards as charismatic cult leader L.Ron Hubbard, the founder of Scientology.

Apparently, Hubbard played a role similar to that of Edward Kelley, "scryer" for the aforementioned Dr. John Dee, of whom Crowley was an ardent admirer. A scryer works as a receptor of otherworldly communications, often using a crystal ball or some similar device in conjunction with the magician's rituals and ceremonies to summon beings from other dimensions. Together, magician and scryer work left hand-in-hand in summoning these otherworldly beings: be they angels, demons or spirits of the dead.

Crowley's Scarlet Woman, in many instances, performed this same function; for instance, Crowley's first wife, Rose Kelly – while in a magical trance – received the first three chapters of the infamous **Book of the Law**, the manuscript that laid the foundation for Crowley's religion, Thelema. Furthermore, the portal of entry for the extraterrestrial beings that Crowley theoretically opened (when he invoked the entity "Lam") may have been further enlarged by Parsons and Hubbard with the commencement of the Babalon Working, thus facilitating a monumental paradigm shift in human consciousness. As Kenneth Grant wrote, "The [Babalon] Working began...just prior to the wave of unexplained aerial phenomena now recalled as the 'Great Flying Saucer Flap.' Parsons opened a door and something flew in." Such researchers as John Carter suggest that the detonation of atomic bombs over Japan during the latter part of World War II may have also played a part in opening this door between dimensions or, at the least, attracted the curiosity of our intergalactic neighbors.

As Thelemic history instructs, 1947 ended the first stage of the Babalon Working, as Parsons and Hubbard parted ways after a falling out. (Apparently, Hubbard ran off with Parsons' wife and a large part of his fortune.) It was the same year the Modern Age of UFOs began with the Kenneth Arnold sightings over Mt. Rainer in Washington State, followed not long after by the alleged saucer crash in Roswell, New Mexico.

1947 was also the year that marked the passing of The Great Beast, Aleister Crowley. Not long after these monumental events, in 1948, Albert Hoffman gave birth to LSD, which indicates that strange things were indeed afoot in the collective unconscious of humanity between the years of 1946–'48. Connecting all this high weirdness up even tighter is conspiracy researcher John Judge, who – in an interview on KPFK radio, Los Angeles, on August 12, 1989, dubbed "Unidentified Fascist Observatories" – stated that Kenneth Arnold and Jack Parsons were flying partners, though I have, as yet, been unable to find additional corroboration to support this claim.

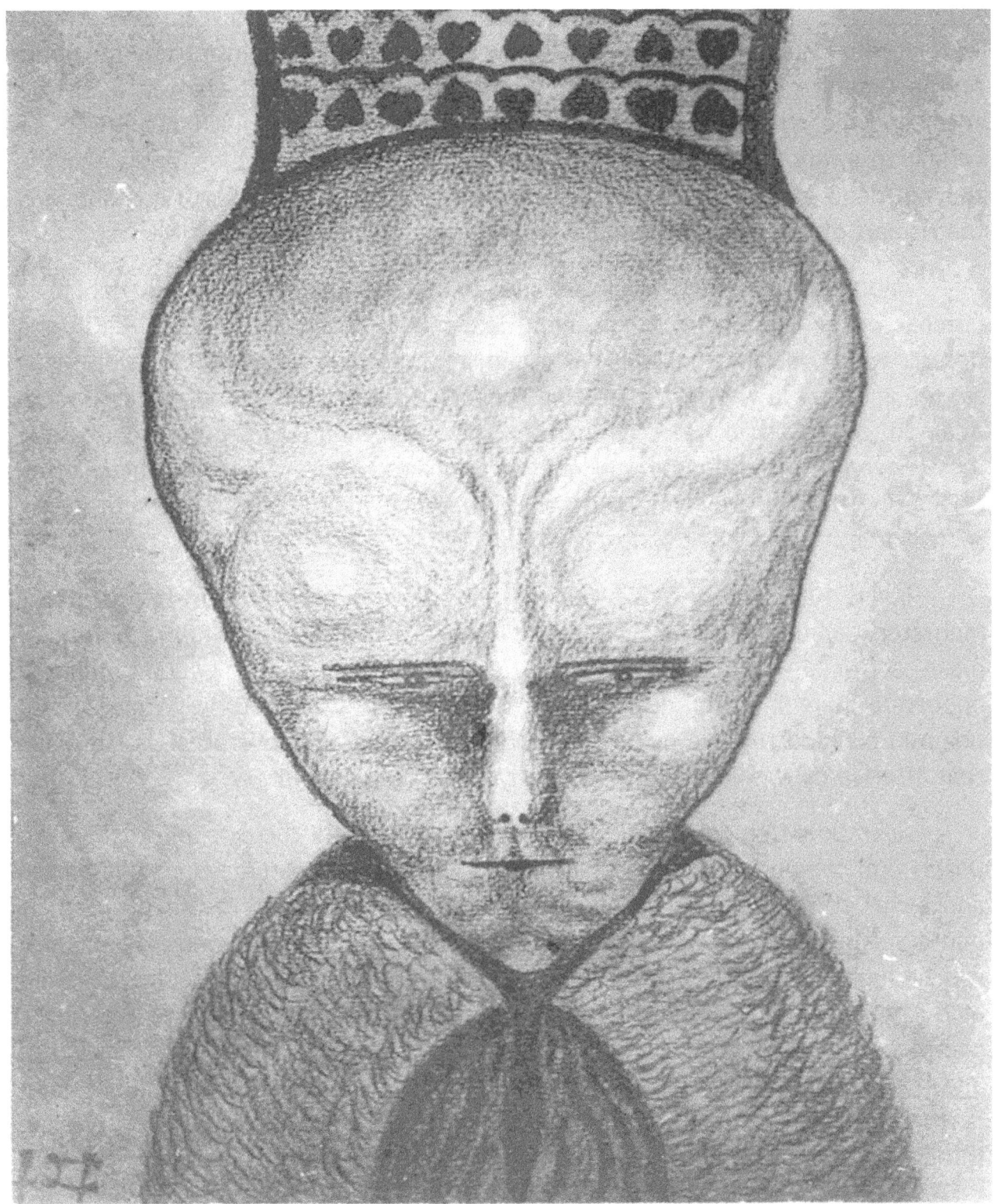

"Lam" by Aleister Crowley. His note under it reads: "Lam is the Tibetan word for Way or Path, and Lama is He who Goeth, the specific title of the Gods of Egypt, the Treader of the Path, in Buddhistic phraseology."

As for L. Ron Hubbard – though it is not well publicized by current day members of the Church of Scientology – much of his "religion" was based on a bizarre cosmology he apparently concocted, perhaps to see how much his flock was willing to swallow; a thesis which suggested that several million years ago the souls of dead space aliens (Thetans) entered into the body of Earth humans, and that is part of the reason why today we are so screwed up as a species.

Another interesting "UFO" parallel to note is that Parsons and Hubbard's visionary experience with these alien-like entities transpired in the California desert, which, during the late 1940s and into the 50s, was a hotbed for flying saucer activity. It was in this setting that such famous "Contactees" as George Adamski and George Hunt Williamson invoked their own brand of cosmic messengers, transported by saucers, cigar-shaped vessels and the like, often originating from nearby Venus or other seemingly uninhabitable planets in our solar system.

In the 1930s – prior to his "Space Brother" encounters – Adamski operated a monastery dubbed "The Royal Order of Tibet," which afforded him a permit to make sacrificial wine during the Prohibition. After the Prohibition ended, Adamski opened a burger stand near the Mount Palomar Observatory. While there, Adamski claimed to have helped astronomers photograph several UFOs – a claim that afterwards was never verified by anyone at the observatory.

Adamski's first encounter with the "Space Brothers" occurred in the Mojave Desert on November 20, 1952, when – in the company of George Hunt Williamson and some other friends – he witnessed a cigar-shaped craft being pursued by military jets. Just before disappearing from sight, the craft ejected a silver disc, which landed a short distance from Adamski and his party. When Adamski arrived at the saucer he was greeted by a man with long blond hair who was wearing a one-piece suit. Telepathically, the "man" informed Adamski he was from Venus and that he was concerned about the possibility of atomic bomb radiation from Earth reaching other planets in the solar system and that various beings from throughout the galaxy were visiting Earth harboring these same concerns.

According to Adamski, he was taken aboard one of the alien ships and flown around to several venues throughout the universe, including the dark side of the moon. During the course of his aerial foray, Adamski took an array of spurious photographs that have been widely viewed as a hoax. In "Unidentified Fascist

Observatories" John Judge asserts that Adamski was an asset of the CIA, who in his lecture tours throughout the 1950s and 60's dispersed disinfo on behalf of the Company.

Adamski's colleague, George Hunt Williamson, went on to author several UFO books, such as **Other Tongues - Other Flesh**, and promulgated the idea of a cosmic good-versus-evil battle taking place between the "good guys" from the dog star, Sirius, versus the evil shit-kickers from Orion. Strangely enough, the planet Sirius is a recurring theme found throughout occult and UFO lore.

Of note in this regard is Robert Temple's **The Sirius Mystery**, published in 1977, which documents the history of the Dogon tribe of Africa and their fabled meetings with the Nommos, a race of three-eyed, crab-clawed beings from Sirius. It was these intergalactic emissaries – as Dogon legends record – that passed onto the tribe as far back as 3200 B.C. various astronomical data instructing them that Sirius had a companion star invisible to the naked eye. These legends far predate the advent of telescopes, and were later confirmed by astronomers. This "companion" star – Sirius B – wasn't even photographed until 1970. In addition to this knowledge regarding Sirius B, the Nommos also provided additional info to the Dogons; such as the fact that Jupiter has four moons, Saturn has a ring around it, and that the planets in our solar system orbit around the sun. All of these facts were later confirmed by science.

In **The Sirius Mystery**, Temple traces contact with the Nommos all the way back to Sumeria circa 4500 B.C. At that time, he says, these three-eyed-crab-clawed creatures appeared in their mighty space ships from the stars, bestowing unto humankind vast secrets; revealing mysteries and esoteric knowledge passed on to initiates in various secret societies in Egypt, the Near East, and Greece. These initial contacts, Temple contends, planted the seeds for the various mystery religions, whose offshoots include the likes of Giordano Bruno, Dr. John Dee, and the overall foundation which laid the stones for Freemasonry, and other secret schools of esoteric knowledge such as The Knights Templar and the Rosicrucians. In fact, Freemasons believe that civilization on Earth was initially formed by entities from the Sirius star system, whom they equate with the Egyptian Trinity of Isis, Osiris, and Horus. In these legends, Osiris has been portrayed as a precursor to Christ, who was first crucified then later resurrected, forming the basis of an Egyptian priesthood that worships Sun gods. The adepts of these mystery religions have always referred to themselves, in one form or another, as The Illuminati – those who have been "illuminated" by their worship of the various Sun gods/Moon goddesses.

In his treatise, Temple further notes that the entire Egyptian calendar revolved around the movements of Sirius, and that the calendar year began with the "dog days" when Sirius started to rise behind the sun. According to Philip Vandenberg in *The Curse of the Pharaoh*: "An archeologist named Duncan MacNaughton discovered in 1932 that the long dark tunnels in the Great Pyramid of Cheops function as telescopes, making the stars visible even in the daytime. The Greater Pyramid is oriented, according to MacNaughton, to give a view, from the King's Chamber, of the area of the southern sky in which Sirius moves throughout the year."

The brightest star in the heavens, Sirius is approximately 35 times brighter than our own sun and is regarded in occult circles as the "hidden god of the cosmos." The famous emblem of the all-seeing eye, hovering above the unfinished pyramid, is a depiction of the Eye of Sirius, a common motif found throughout Masonic lore. It is no secret that many of our nation's founding fathers were Freemasons, which explains the odd appearance of the Eye of Sirius on the dollar bill; a symbol seen every day by millions of people, imprinting its image forever in our psyches. The imprinting of such imagery has been called into question in recent times by a whole host of conspiracy theorists, who – in their New World Order scenarios – connect such fraternal orders as the Knights of Malta, Freemasonry and Rosicrucianism with the "insidious" symbol of Sirius, the eye in the triangle. At the top of this pyramid – the conspiracy theorists contend – is the dreaded Illuminati, tying all of these fraternal orders and secret societies together in a far-flung plot intended to bring mankind to its knees under a futuristic Orwellian nightmare; a totalitarian society masquerading as a libertarian democracy, which uses Masonic imagery to program the masses.

And if this entire story wasn't already jumbled enough, the dawning of the 20th century ushered in a new generation of contactees paying homage to the "Dog Star," expounding ever further upon the legend of the hovering eye atop the pyramid. Right around the turn of the century, a gentleman named Lucien-Francois Jean-Maine formed an order in Haiti called the Cult of the Black Snake that used rituals borrowed from Crowley's O.T.O. in combination with certain voodoo practices. In 1922, these rituals reportedly summoned forth a disembodied being named Lam, the very same entity that Aleister Crowley made contact with a few years earlier. In fact, Kenneth Grant has stated that Crowley "unequivocally identifies his Holy Guardian Angel with Sothis (Sirius), or Set-Isis."

Later, in the 1950s and 60s, the aforementioned saucer "Contactee," George Hunt Williamson, once again summoned forth certain denizens purportedly from Sirius, conversing to them in the same "Enochian" or "angelic" language used by Dr. John Dee and Aleister Crowley. In his various books and lectures, Williamson also spoke of a secret society on Earth that has been in contact with Sirius for thousands of years, and that the emblem of this secret society is the eye of Horus, otherwise known as the all-seeing eye.

As previously noted, Williamson was a close associate of George Adamski, perhaps the most famous of the early UFO Contactees, who claimed to be connected with astronomers at Palomar Observatory in California, in whose company he allegedly witnessed several UFO sightings. In an essay entitled *"Sorcery, Sex, Assassination, and the Science of Symbolism,"* author James Shelby Downard describes a "Sirius-worship cult" reaching all the way to the highest levels of the CIA. In this provocative piece, Downard describes one of their rituals taking place at the Palomar Observatory under the telescopically focused light of Sirius, bathing its participants in the luminance of the majestic Dog-Star.

A rash of Sirian references continued on into the 1970s, perhaps inspired by Robert Temple's book. In 1974, science fiction writer Phillip K. Dick had some sort of "mystical experience" which at first he attributed to psychotronic transmissions broadcast from Russia. According to Dick, these "micro-wave boosted telepathic transmissions," as he called them, commenced on March 20, 1974, showering him with streams of visual and audio data. Initially, this overpowering onslaught of messages that Dick received was extremely unpleasant and, as he termed them, "die messages." Within the following week, he reported being kept awake by "violet phosphene activity, eight hours uninterrupted." A description of this event in a fictionalized form appears in Dick's ***A Scanner, Darkly***. The content of this phosphene activity was in the form of modern abstract graphics followed by Soviet music serenading his head, in addition to Russian names and words. Dick's original theory was that Russian mind control agents were targeting him with these transmissions.

At the outset, Dick felt the emanations invading his mind were of a malevolent nature, although in time he began to believe they were something entirely different. In a letter to Ira Einhorn, dated February 10, 1978, Dick went into more depth on these psychotronic transmissions, claiming that they "seemed sentient." He felt that an alien life form existing in some upper layer of the Earth's atmosphere had been attracted by the Soviet psychotronic transmissions. Apparently, this alien life form operated as a "station," tapping into some sort of interplanetary communication grid that, "...contained and transmitted vast amounts of information."

What Dick initially received were the Soviet transmissions, but eventually this alien life form – whom he called Zebra – became "attracted or potentiated by the Soviet microwave psychotronic transmissions." In the months that followed, this alien entity – according to Dick – vastly improved his mental and physical well-being in a number of ways. It (Zebra) gave him "complex and accurate information about myself and also about our infant son, which, Zebra said, had a critical and undiagnosed birth defect which required emergency and immediate surgery. My wife rushed our baby to the doctor and told the doctor what I had said (more precisely what Zebra had said to me) and the doctor discovered that it was so. Surgery was scheduled for the following day – i.e. as soon as possible. Our son would have died otherwise." (Dick's wife Tessa and others have since confirmed this story regarding the medical conditions of himself and his son, Christopher.)

Phil Dick felt Zebra was totally benign, and it held great contempt for the Soviets and their psychotronic experiments. Furthermore, Zebra informed Dick that the Earth was dying, and that spray-cans were "destroying the layer of atmosphere in which Zebra…existed."

It was not until several years after his "mystical experiences" with Zebra that Phil Dick finally wrote about these events in his classic novel, *VALIS*. Prior to the publication of *VALIS*, Dick had never made any mention of Sirius in connection with the events that so drastically impacted his life. However, in this classic work, Dick renamed Zebra to VALIS (Vast Active Living Intelligence System) and identified it as a product of the Sirius star system, identifying its operators as three-eyed crab-clawed beings.

PROJECT ALIEN MIND CONTROL -- UFO REVIEW SPECIAL

During this same period – 1973-74 – Robert Anton Wilson was having his own experiences with "ET denizens" which at the time he thought were "telepathic communications from Sirius," as recounted in his mind-blowing book, *Cosmic Trigger*. Also in the early 70s, English mainstream novelist Doris Lessing began a series of Sci-Fi novels revolving around entities from Sirius, which was a definite departure from her previous literary offerings. In the third novel of this series, *The Sirian Experiments*, Lessing relates a tale with stunning similarities to Dick's VALIS experiences. When Robert Anton Wilson met Ms. Lessing in 1983, she said she had never read a lick of Dick, or Wilson, for that matter, so it's hard to tell whether much of this was cross-pollination; be it intentional or a subconscious filtration process that leaked in and out of a few brains fixated on The Dog Star.

Another somewhat unlikely source for such conjecture was the heavy metal rock band Blue Oyster Cult. At face value, one might consider BOC another in a long line of head banging guitar slingers, but upon closer examination many of their lyrics allude to subjects occult and arcane, often referring to amphibian-like beings from outer space as well as Sirius in their song "Astronomy": "...and don't forget my dog, fixed and consequent. Astronomy...a star!"

But not only has Sirius cropped up time and again in occult and UFO lore, but the ubiquitous Dog Star has also been mentioned in relation to certain mind control experiments which fall under the nefarious umbrella of the CIA's MK-ULTRA project. Purportedly started in 1953 – under a program that was exempt from congressional oversight – MK-ULTRA agents and "spychiatrists" tested radiation, electric shock, microwaves and electrode implants on unwitting subjects. The ultimate goal of MK-ULTRA was to create programmed assassins ala "The Manchurian Candidate." The CIA also tested a wide range of drugs in the prospects of discovering the perfect chemical compound to control minds. LSD was one such drug that deeply interested CIA spychiatrists, so much so that in 1953 the Agency attempted to purchase the entire world supply of acid from Sandoz Laboratories in Switzerland. In fact, for many years the CIA was the principal source for LSD.

In recent years, various info on remote mind control technology has filtered into the conspiracy research community through "alternative" publications such as *"Full Disclosure"* and *"Resonance,"* as well as a Finnish gentleman by the name of Martti Koski and his booklet, *My Life Depends On You.* Over the last decade, Mr. Koski has been sharing his horrifying tale, documenting as it does the discovery of rampant brain tampering committed upon himself and countless others. The perpetrators of these evil doings allegedly include the Royal Canadian Mounted Police, the CIA and Finnish Intelligence, among various other intelligence agencies. Where Sirius comes into the clouded picture is quite interesting: at one point during a mind control programming episode, the "doctors" operating on Koski identified themselves as "aliens from Sirius." Apparently, these "doctors" (or "spychiatrists") were attempting to plant a screen memory to conceal their true intentions. What this suggests is a theory that a handful of researchers – namely Martin Cannon, Alex Constantine, David Emory and John Judge – started kicking around in the early 1990s: that Alien Abductions were a cover for MK-ULTRA mind control shenanigans perpetrated by intelligence agency spooks.

According to Walter Bowart, in the revised edition of *Operation Mind Control,* one alleged mind control victim related an incident along these lines, purportedly occurring in the late 70s. In memories retrieved by hypnotic regression, it was revealed that the victim had been the recipient of a mock alien abduction, the intention of which was to create a screen memory that would conceal the actual mind control programs enacted on the victim. The subject in this instance claimed to have seen a young child dressed in a small alien costume, similar in appearance to the aliens in Spielberg's "*ET.*" None of this, of course, dismisses outright the ETH; nor does it mean that ETs have never visited us. Nevertheless, its implications are staggering when one considers the impact and subsequent commercialization of the Alien Abduction Phenomenon, and how it has challenged and reshaped the belief systems and psyches of millions of the planet's inhabitants, in essence creating a new paradigm that prior to thirty years ago was virtually non-existent.

As chronicled in Bowart's *Operation Mind Control*, in the late 70s, Congressman Charlie Rose (D-N.C) met with a Canadian inventor who had developed a helmet that simulated alternate states of consciousness, much like the virtual reality unit in the movie "*Brainstorm*." One such virtual reality scenario played out by those who tried on this helmet was a mock alien abduction. Congressman Rose took part in these experiments, which consisted of this alien abduction scenario. Much to Rose's amazement, the simulated scenario seemed incredibly realistic. This device sounds quite similar to Dr. Michael Persinger's much-touted "Magic Helmet," which has been receiving a fair amount of press in recent years. Equipped with magnets that beam a low-level magnetic field at the temporal lobe, the "Magic Helmet" affects areas of the brain associated with time distortions and other altered states of consciousness. Although Bowart did not specifically name the inventor of the helmet in *Operation Mind Control*, chances are it was Persinger to whom he was referring. Persinger's name has also been bandied about by mind control researcher, Martin Cannon – in his treatise *The Controllers* – as a behind-the-scenes player in MK-ULTRA intelligence operations.

Persinger is a clinical neurophysicist and professor of neuroscience whose work over the years has focused on the effects of electromagnetic fields upon biological organisms and human behavior. Persinger is an adherent to the theory that UFOs are the products of geomagnetic effects released from the Earth's crust under tectonic strain. His "Magic Helmet" – it has been noted – approximates the characteristics of Temporal Lobe Epilepsy (TLE) of which many an armchair theorist have attributed as being responsible for Phil Dick's VALIS experiences. One of the most common attributes of TLE are visions in the form of direct communications with God, or gods – in whatever form – be it aliens, angels, fairies or elves.

Early on in his efforts to explain his own abduction experience, author Whitley Strieber entertained the possibility that he might have been one such victim of TLE. Because of this, Strieber underwent extensive medical examinations, including several CAT scans and MRIs, to determine if such was the case, but the results of all these tests came up negative. Aside from such speculations, there is an undeniable magical component to Whitley Strieber's experiences. After his initial hypnotic regression, when the presence of the "visitors" was first revealed to him, Strieber subsequently practiced a form of meditation to further conjure their image in his mind, so as to better identify their features. The first time he attempted this approach – much to his surprise – an alien grey immediately appeared in his "mental field of view," allowing Strieber to delve deeper into the mystery of the phenomenon. This meditation experience – as recounted in *Communion* – seems nothing less than a magical conjuration, although Strieber may not have been entirely aware of his actions in the context of ritual magic. In a sense, Strieber perhaps performed unconscious magical workings on several occasions, in essence summoning forth these beings from behind the veils of perception.

Furthermore, it is my belief that hypnotic regression can, under certain conditions, perform a sort of magical working, and it was through hypnotic regression that Strieber was able to come to terms with his "visitor experience." Bear in mind that hypnosis approximates a trance state, and it is just this form of altered consciousness that has allowed many an abductee to recall their experiences. Strieber was also, prior to his "visitor" experience, a member of the Gurdjieff Foundation, a self-transformational organization dedicated to a system of techniques devised by the famed mystic G.I. Gurdjieff. As Strieber explained: "I believe that the techniques I learned in that training – particularly a form of double-tone chanting –have enabled me to remain conscious in some experiences with the visitors where I otherwise would have been unconscious." What Strieber doesn't acknowledge is that Gurdjieff himself was in contact with certain denizens of Sirius via this method of double-tone chanting, which could also be described as "Enochian chants."

It was in the early stages of his "visitor" experiences that Strieber made the acquaintance of famed alien abduction investigator Budd Hopkins, who sat in on some of Strieber's early hypnosis sessions. Later, when Strieber was working on the early drafts of **Body Terror** (the original working title of **Communion**), he sent Hopkins excerpts for comment. Hopkins, though he was convinced that Strieber had indeed been visited by alien beings, was somewhat distressed by the amount of high weirdness contained within the manuscript, although there were many parallels with other known abduction cases. During the course of some group abductee meetings attended by Hopkins, Strieber has been quoted as saying that "some people began volunteering stories about having left their bodies or other psychic experiences after their abductions. Budd wasn't interested in that, and would tell people to get back to talking about their abduction experiences. He refused to see a possible link between the experience of abduction and some kind of spiritual or psychic awakening happening in the people to whom experiences occurred."

Elsewhere in **Communion**, Strieber points out that the mental state produced by his encounters with the "visitors" could be approximated by a rare drug called Tetradotoxin, which in small doses causes external anesthesia, and in larger doses may bring about out of body experiences. Even greater doses of the drug can simulate near death experiences. According to Strieber, Tetradotoxin is the core of the zombie poisons of Haiti. What he doesn't mention is that

PROJECT ALIEN MIND CONTROL -- UFO REVIEW SPECIAL

Tetradotoxin was just one in a vast number of psychoactive compounds utilized by the CIA for their infamous MK-ULTRA mind control experiments. Throughout *Communion*, Strieber makes veiled references to mind control (of the MK-ULTRA variety.) At one point in the narrative – as Strieber is haphazardly tossing around various theories regarding his abduction experiences – he brings up the possibility that the alien greys may not have been actually using mental telepathy to communicate, but that something of a more technical nature might have been occurring, such as extra-low-frequency waves beamed into Strieber's brain, thereby producing the requisite "voices in his head."

Along these lines, Strieber adds the interesting aside "that the earth itself generates a good deal of ELF in the 1 to 30 hertz range. Perhaps there are natural conditions that trigger a response in the brain which brings about what is essentially a psychological experience of a rare and powerful kind. Maybe we have a relationship with our own planet that we do not understand at all, and the old gods, the fairies and the modern visitors are side effects of it." Part of the appeal of *Communion* and his subsequent books was, in my opinion, Strieber's ability to entertain a whole host of theories, and in the process open the reader's eyes to the various possibilities attempting to explain the UFO phenomenon, from fairy lore or travelers from alternate dimensions to the very real possibility of some sort of ELF wave/mind control machine being responsible for his haunted reveries.

Inspirational Art of MIB By Carol Ann Rodriguez

PROJECT ALIEN MIND CONTROL -- UFO REVIEW SPECIAL

WHENEVER I am on a talk show discussing the dreaded Men in Black, inevitably I am asked the hundred thousand dollar question: Who are the Men in Black? Are they government agents or radical ETs looking to cause chaos and confusion in an attempt to silence an individual who may have seen or found out too much about the UFO situation at hand?

For many years I stumbled and stuttered out any kind of answer, even if it was an illogical one, not knowing really what to say or how to hedge my bet as to who – or *what* – were behind the dozens of MIB capers that were being called to my attention. The MIB cases that I was hearing about seemed to come in "waves," followed by prolonged dry periods when these denizens of darkness seem to have gone back underground.

Recently the reports started to heat up again!

They were centering on the state of Iowa and were initially bought to my attention by my friends and colleagues, Brad and Sherry Steiger.

Addressing me as "Brother Tim," the missive went something like this: "Facebook and YouTube are crowing over MIBs. The first sighting apparently was made by a R.J. Strong of Port Louisa on or around June 13 (2016) at 2 AM as he was driving near Ogilvie Avenue in Muscatine County. He told the local TV station, KWQC, that some 'weirdo was walking down the center of the paved road in a long, black trench coat.'"

The local Sheriff's office said they had received maybe about six reports of similarly clad individuals either walking down the road or standing perched at the shoulder as if ready to pounce on their pray (passing motorists?).

"My son has experienced this and it's no joke," posted Beatrice Wilson Strong. "It was really a frightening experience to him."

Likewise, Cassie Pameticky posted on Facebook, "It's happened to a few friends of mine out on [Highway] 22."

This comes on the heels of West Quincy, Iowa, resident Jordan Law, who saw what she thought were two human bodies lying on the side of the road. She pulled over right away and called the police. Then the two "bodies" got up and started running after her.

This incident has been put down as a teenagers' prank, but the Muscatine County Sheriff's Office has taken notice, posting Monday on its Facebook page, "We have had several reports of 'men dressed in black' entering the roadway in rural Muscatine County."

Chicago's Channel 5 News added this report from an eyewitness. "My wife, mother in-law, and I were headed home on Highway 22 at 10:30 PM on June 15th, headed towards Muscatine from Quad Cities, and just past the big hill past Fairport. As we got just past the cabins, there was someone all in white with either white makeup on or a thin white mask lying in the ditch right by the road, and he sat up with his thumb up." The witness said he figured it was a mannequin at first, but when he returned later, it was gone.

It has also been noted that these same individuals have been spotted walking across homeowners' yards, on private property.

The MCSO is now asking anyone who encounters the individuals to "call 911 immediately."

The sheriff's Facebook post has generated several jokes and speculation that harmless pranksters are behind the sightings.

However, the MCSO says on its Facebook page, "We do take this seriously," and investigators are "hoping the public can assist."

ON PHANTOMS AND MONSTERS

Unfortunately, it is almost unprecedented for any local media to carry MIB reports, save for the Mothman flap in Point Pleasant, West Virginia, way back in the 1960s, so in order to get additional details one has to depend upon the Internet or one's own independent sources.

Hardly a day goes by when *On Phantoms and Monsters* doesn't add a substantial amount of new material pertaining to whatever is trending at the time. The recent MIB reports out of Iowa wasn't any different than, say, the Dogman cases that have updated their site a few days previously. As an example, this is what Craig C. posted:

> "I got an email from a friend about a happening south of Iowa City around Muscatin, Iowa.

What are we to make of the origins for the MIB? Are they earthly? Extraterrestrial? Or somewhere "in-between"?

PROJECT ALIEN MIND CONTROL -- UFO REVIEW SPECIAL

"The occurrence is from last Thursday: June 17th, 2016. Not sure if it's just pranksters or something else, but the following is what I got:

"Last night, around 10:50 PM, 'George' was driving home and experienced something really creepy. He was driving along Highway 22, just before Hon Geneva, when he saw a strange, tall man, dressed all in black step out from the ditch on to the side of the highway. As George passed him, the man stepped out from behind his car, into the middle of his lane, and stopped and watched him drive off. (As George described, the man cocked his head to the side while he watched him drive away and his arms weren't down against his sides, more curved as if he were holding basketballs under his wrists against his hips. Maybe to appear stronger in stature.) He said his face was black too. Maybe painted or a mask, but he could not make out facial features. A bit shaken, he continued driving towards home when a second man (clothed the same way and same demeanor) stepped out from the ditch just before Sweetland Road. At this point, George floored the gas and sped home. When he came in the door he was distraught. Listening to him tell me about his encounter scared me. I reported the men to the sheriff. Alan took George back out to look for the men but never saw them again. The sheriff called and asked to meet with George about this in the last month. There have been sightings of the same thing near Fairport. I am posting this because I want to warn all of you that live along the highway or drive along 22 at night to keep a lookout. Not sure what they are up to, but it's creepy!"

To my way of thinking, it's kind of a crazy, somewhat confusing timeline of the MIB activity. Unless there were a group of them, they seem to have spread out over the landscape pretty far and wide – and for what purpose?

Tim Swartz told me that, in his preparation to appear on Clyde Lewis' "Ground Zero" program, he discovered that there had been some limited UFO activity in Iowa just before the appearance of the MIBs. A report filed with the Mutual UFO Network lists a sighting of a UFO complete with a row of windows. Several "fireballs" were also seen, though no details are displayed on the *UFO Hunters* site.

WHAT OF THEIR ORIGINS?

But getting back to square one – previewed before the MIB update – what are we to make of the origins for the MIB? Are they earthly? Extraterrestrial? Or somewhere "in-between"? As astute researcher/author Nick Redfern has pointed out, we have considered what would seem like all the various possibilities, "including aliens, government agents, time-travelers, and dimension-hoppers." There is, however, at least one other possible theory that is scarcely considered. And it just so happens to be a theory I purposed to Nick some months previous to his public statement on the subject.

"What if the MIB are not extraterrestrials, time-surfers from the distant future, agents of officialdom, or inter-dimensional creatures? What if, incredibly, they are normal, everyday people, just like me and you? Or, to put it more correctly, what if they are everyday people most of the time? Could it be the case that the MIB are regular individuals who, now and again, become possessed by a paranormal force – a demonic force – some might even suggest – that uses those poor souls as vessels to perform tasks of the terrifying kind?

"To some, it may sound not just controversial, but beyond controversial. But, don't be so quick to write-off just such a possibility. One case in particular suggests that that may be exactly what is going on. And, for the answers to that case we have to turn our attentions to a longtime researcher of the UFO mystery: Timothy Green Beckley. Beckley's research suggests that the Men in Black may actually be regular individuals who have been placed under a form of mind-control, very much akin (in slave-like behavior, at least) to the kind of zombification that appears within Haitian lore."

Thinking back, I had apparently spoken to Nick about a highly frightening, ongoing series of threats by someone I had met at the office of an individual who was at the time publishing a nationally distributed newsstand magazine on UFOs. The magazine had printed several narratives detailing close encounters with the MIB.

I wrote for this publication in the 1970s; it was called *Official UFO*. They always published their address in the magazine, so they did get a few crank visitors to their offices. They also published dozens of other, non-UFO type, magazines. One day, while I was there on other publishing business, there was this gentleman who showed up claiming he was being stalked by the Men in Black. The fellow was disheveled in appearance, rambling wildly, and kept scratching as if he were being repeatedly bitten by insects. I tried my best to ignore him as I knew that something was "just not right" about him.

Unfortunately, not too long afterward, I actually encountered the man in the street. He seemed to block my path. There was a glazed look in his eyes as if he could go ballistic at any moment. I excused myself as quickly as possible, and thus began a disturbing series of events that lasted across the late 1970s and early 1980s – during which time I received a series of disturbing and chilling phone calls from the man.

They were so chilling and disturbing – never mind threatening, too – that I finally chose to contact the police. It didn't take the NYC police long to find the man; he was living on the streets and sleeping somewhere in Grand Central Terminal, around Times Square.

I explained that this creepy character must have called fifty times and left crazy, threatening messages that would go on and on – and not only had he threatened me, but also several local politicians and a female DJ who he was stalking on the side. I told the police I had even spoken with his parents (he was a grown man in his forties) – who were in Florida – and they said that although he wasn't always like this, something came over him "now and again." On one occasion he had even held a knife at his brother's throat.

I began to notice this pattern over and over again, how these individuals – usually on the margins of society – were going into trance-like states, only to find their already surly disposition becoming far worse, to the point of hostility. This individual kept saying that he knew the astronomer Dr. Morris K. Jessup who had, of course, committed apparent suicide years before. From what I could see, he was taking on the character of a MIB. He was lock-jawed and zombie-like, repeating his threats over and over.

There is no doubt that he was possessed, under "someone's" spell. Some paranormal force takes hold of the person and they become a literal Man in Black, doing what the "outside force" wants them to do, but without their knowledge of their own behavior in most instances. Afterwards, they might not even remember any of what had occurred. These folks are living on the fringe of our society as it is; they are usually very simple-minded people who can very easily be manipulated and influenced. Someone, say, who might be living in some rundown apartment, is taken over in a sort of enchantment, and then becomes one of the Men in Black for a period of time. They threaten someone and then they go back to their normal life after the possession ends, unable to recall this schizophrenic episode. But while they are under the control of whatever is doing this, they're not "quite right." It's like being a full-blown zombie, which is the best way I can describe this state or mental condition.

Putting his stretchable, woolen thinking cap on, Nick Redfern sort of reinforces my position, taking a few elements from the theory I have developed.

"Beckley's description is certainly a highly apt one: George Romero's cannibalistic zombies in *Night of the Living Dead* – and, indeed in *all* of Romero's subsequent movies in the still-ongoing *Dead* series – are utterly driven by two issues: the desire for self-preservation, and an unrelenting need to feed. The MIB are equally and similarly driven; however, their whole goal is to instill fear rather than feed upon flesh and bone. But, just like the reanimated dead of the big-screen, the Men in Black, too, appear to lack anything more than a basic awareness of why, precisely, they are carrying out the actions they dutifully and never-endingly perform. Might that be due to paranormal possession? Demonic possession, perhaps? It may not be wise to dismiss either scenario..."

Going a step further, in the next presented scenario, Redfern shows us that not all MIB are, actually, Men in Black, and that we have to deal with the female side of the phenomenon as well.

MIND CONTROL AND THE WOMEN IN BLACK

Not All MIBs Are Zombified Men Dressed Entirely in Black. Many of These "Cloaked Figures" Can Be Readily Identified As Members Of A Sort Of Sinister Alien Sisterhood.

By Nick Redfern

PROJECT ALIEN MIND CONTROL -- UFO REVIEW SPECIAL

ON October 23, 1971, the U.S. media reported on a very strange story:

"A part-time housekeeper at President Nixon's Key Biscayne retreat has testified she was put in a hypnotic daze by a stranger who told her to shoplift four dresses. Shirley Cromartie, 32, and a mother of three, pleaded no contest Thursday and was given a suspended sentence after law enforcement officers and a psychiatrist testified they believed she was telling the truth. Mrs. Cromartie holds a security clearance to work in the Florida White House, according to testimony. She said a woman met her in a parking lot and asked the time, then ordered her to take the items and bring them to her.

"Mrs. Cromartie testified she fell into a daze when the young woman released a jasmine-like scent from her left hand. 'I just sort of lost my will ... it was a terrifying experience,' she testified. Mrs. Cromartie joined the Key Biscayne White House housekeeping staff about a year ago, according to FBI Agent Leo Mc Clairen. He testified her background was impeccable.

"Dr. Albert Jaslow, a psychiatrist, said he examined her and found she could be hypnotized 'quickly and easily' and believed she was telling the truth. 'But it wasn't the same when he hypnotized me,' Mrs. Cromartie said. 'I couldn't remember anything afterwards. Whatever that young woman did to me, it was like being in a sleepwalk, only awake.'"

As the media continued to dig into the story, things got even stranger. The mysterious woman, with the mind-altering, "jasmine-like scent," was described as being attractive, young, dressed completely in black, and wearing a wig – the latter being something which is a staple part of certain Women in Black cases. Also, both the WIB and the MIB are oddly fond of asking people the time, as Cromartie's mysterious woman was so very careful to do.

Metro Court Judge Frederick Barad said of this surreal saga: "This is all so bizarre that I'm frightened what could happen to the president."

This latter point was something clearly on the mind of John Keel, too. He speculated that the hypnotic abilities of Cromartie's wig-wearing WIB amounted to "...not some small demonstration for the benefit of President Nixon."

Almost certainly, "the jasmine-like scent" was a substance that is known officially as scopolamine, but which has a far more ominous slang name: "The Devil's Breath." It is synthesized from the Borrachero Tree, which grows widely in Colombia. Aside from its jasmine-like odor, scopolamine is a powerful drug, exposure to which can almost instantaneously take away a person's free-will, self-preservation, and self-control. To demonstrate its power, there are accounts – from Colombia - of people exposed to scopolamine emptying their bank-accounts and handing over their precious savings to criminals using the drug against unwitting souls. It's no wonder, then, that Mrs. Cromartie acted in such a strange, detached, and atypical fashion. But that's not all.

The CIA made great use of scopolamine at the height of the Cold War, using it on captured Soviet spies and defecting agents. Britain's intelligence agency, MI6, has even been rumored to have used scopolamine to provoke troublesome characters - those having a bearing on national security issues - into committing suicide. That Mrs. Cromartie worked for the U.S. Government – and for no less a personage than the President of the United States – makes one wonder if there was some sort of presently unclear connection between her experience, the Nixon administration, and the secret CIA world of scopolamine use and manipulation of the human mind.

There is another side to this story. Many people who have encountered the WIB have stated that although these entities are generally highly attractive, there is something about them – something intangible, hard to define, yet downright sinister – that makes people want to avoid them, and at just about all costs possible. As we have seen, however, there are cases where men, despite having alarm bells ringing in their heads telling them to run like hell, became entranced and obsessed by the WIB they crossed paths with. It transpires that ancient folklore tells of how jasmine has aphrodisiac properties and can be used to not only increase libido, but also to entice a man to become overwhelmingly attracted to one particular woman, almost in slave-like fashion.

Was Shirley Cromartie's WIB an agent of the CIA, using her skills in some strange program that, as John Keel said, was intended as "not some small demonstration for the benefit of President Nixon?" On the other hand, perhaps she was nothing stranger than an opportunist criminal, dosing Cromartie with scopolamine as a means to use her to commit an act of shoplifting. It's worth noting, however, that just like so many other black-garbed WIB she (A) wore a wig, (B) asked Cromartie the time (something the MIB regularly do), and (C) attracted the attention of Keel, which leaves wide open the possibility that the woman was far worse than anything that could come out of the criminal underworld of Colombia or the confines of the CIA. A true WIB, she just may have been.

On this latter point, there is yet *another* issue that links President Nixon and the Women in Black. In 1971, the very same year that Shirley Cromartie – an employee of the Nixon administration, as we have seen – ended up in hot water with the police as a result of her WIB encounter, Nixon himself had a meeting in the White House's Oval Office with a famous psychic named Jeane Dixon. President Nixon, via his personal secretary, Rose Mary Woods, was kept abreast of Dixon's claimed psychic predictions, which reportedly included the November 22, 1963 assassination of President John F. Kennedy and a terrorist attack on the Munich, Germany, Olympics in September 1972.

It so transpires that Dixon (who provided astrological readings for Nancy Reagan, when her husband, Ronald Reagan, was president) asserted that her psychic skills were bestowed upon her by none other than "a wandering Gypsy lady." She was very much like a presumed gypsy who turned up at an isolated farmhouse near Melville, New York, in early 1967, and who scared the living daylights out of the UFO witness who made the unfortunate and rash decision to open his front door to her.

That Dixon developed her powers after meeting a female "gypsy," that both Nixon and Reagan had close links to Dixon, and that one of Nixon's staff had an encounter with a very chilling Woman in Black, suggests something ominous: a potential plan on the part of the WIB to try and infiltrate none other than the Oval Office itself, via nothing less than mind-control.

PROJECT ALIEN MIND CONTROL -- UFO REVIEW SPECIAL

BEFORE we dismiss the idea that aliens can control human minds as "too far-fetched," we should bear in mind that stories involving some kind of "demonic possession" go back for thousands of years.

The Pagan Gnostics believed that malevolent "Archons" could take control of human minds, and, throughout all belief systems, similar influences are described under a variety of different names including demons, djinns, shedim, asuras and more. The belief in external evil beings that can possess humanity is ubiquitous. Truth, they say, is stranger than fiction, and the case history we are about to examine postulates that these influences are alien – in the literal sense.

CHILLING REPORT OF A PROCESS LEADING TO POSSESSION

In his recently published biographical account, author and academic Raymond Samuels II recounts his personal experience of what he believes can only be described as alien influences within his own family. Certain behaviors are completely alien to any normal human mind-set, and Samuels has seen members of his family fall under influences that have torn the family apart. Most disturbing of all, he believes that the alien influence revels in inflicting suffering through its control of human hosts.

PROJECT ALIEN MIND CONTROL -- UFO REVIEW SPECIAL

MAN ENCOUNTERS ALIENS, BECOMES MONSTER

It all began when Horace Carby-Samuels described encounters with aliens when in a dream-like state which he described as "near-death experiences" to Raymond Samuels, whose interest in alien encounters had led him to do extensive research and journalistic work on the matter. Many individuals who have experienced alien encounters report similar experiences to those reported by Carby-Samuels, and these have invariably had frightening negative consequences.

Fearing for his father's well-being, Raymond Samuels warned that these alien encounters should be resisted at all costs. But Horace Carby-Samuels' sense of reality appeared to deteriorate rapidly and he began to rave about "demons." At the same time, Samuels began to notice a similar deterioration in the psychological state of his sister, Marcella Carby-Samuels.

WHEN HUMANS BECOME INHUMAN

Through his previous research, Samuels had observed that victims of alien encounters often begin to indulge in sadistic behaviors, and, to his dismay, he became the helpless witness to an "ultimate sacrifice" targeting his mother.

The frail, elderly woman was denied food on a regular basis and was denied access to a doctor who had successfully been treating her medical condition. Samuels tried to intervene, taking on the role of care-giver, but Horace Carby Samuels and Marcella Carby-Samuels conspired in a plot that would see fabricated evidence being used to deny him access to the family home.

As the victim's condition deteriorated at an alarming rate as a result of abuse and neglect, Samuels attempted to invoke the aid of social services, but, within a short time, even social workers were barred from access to his mother.

THE ULTIMATE SACRIFICE: YOUR OWN MOTHER

Marcella's involvement in this situation is most shocking of all. She is well aware of the deterioration in her mother's condition, but seems determined to support Carby-Samels' abuse of his wife. The once active elderly woman is now unable to speak or walk, and her single written plea for help has been rejected by authorities.

Medical recommendations for therapy that might relieve her mother's distress to some degree have been summarily rejected with Marcella's acquiescence, and the only doctor who has access to the ailing woman has a particularly bad reputation. However, Marcella remains steadfast in her support of conditions that inflict unnecessary suffering on her own mother. Samuels believes that the only possible explanation for this behavior is that she is sacrificing her mother to her new "masters."

FAMILY DISPUTE OR EVIL INFLUENCE?

To an outsider, Samuels' situation may seem like a simple family dispute and a sad account of elder abuse, but in his book *"Unimaginable Evil: The Unauthorized Biographies of Marcella Carby-Samuels and Horace Carby-Samuels"* (ISBN 978-1-927538-04-3), Samuels investigates the findings of other authorities who have studied alien activities and who have also concluded that sadism and the possession of willing minds are characteristics that require their interventions.

The book will be a thought-provoking read – for those who believe that aliens affect our daily lives and skeptics alike. The work of respected authorities such as Dr. Michael Salla and David Icke, appear to support Samuels's conclusions, and this first-hand account of alien involvement in a family's situation makes for gripping though harrowing reading.

Posted In *The Canadian Guardian*

EDITED BY PAULETTE LANGLOIS

The Pagan Gnostics believed that malevolent "Archons" could take control of human minds, and, throughout all belief systems, similar influences are described under a variety of different names including demons, djinns, shedim, asuras and more.

PROJECT ALIEN MIND CONTROL -- UFO REVIEW SPECIAL

AT the time of the incidents in 1980, Maria Korn was a 14-year-old boarder at the Convent of Jesus and Mary in Milton Keynes, Buckinghamshire, Great Britain. As reported by researcher Robert Bull, Maria was receiving psychological counseling from a Dr Black for acute anorexia and sleeping difficulties.

One night Maria couldn't sleep and got up, at about 1:00 AM to look at the stars. She stood by the window overlooking the tennis court and was surprised to see a large, ball-shaped flashing light inside the tennis court itself, which was completely surrounded by wire netting.

She looked at it for about five minutes, and then turned away. When she looked again at about 1:30 AM the object had gone, but she heard a strange whirring sound and, looking up, she saw the object again just above the window, but there were no lights on it this time. The object then moved off rapidly.

The next morning, none of the other girls mentioned having seen anything strange during the night, and Maria kept her experience to herself. Later that morning she was playing tennis when she slipped and fell, and was surprised to see a large, shallow, circular depression seemingly burnt onto the tennis court, exactly where she had seen the object the night before. The next day the police arrived to inspect the damage, but Maria didn't tell anyone what she had seen two nights before.

Three or four months later Maria was in a math class when one of the nuns, Sister Jennifer, interrupted the class and took her out, saying that she had a visitor. Maria thought at the time that it was unusual for the class to be interrupted, visitors normally came only at weekends, and she was worried in case the visitor was bringing bad news.

Sister Jennifer showed her into a dining room where, sitting at a large table, was not one visitor but two men dressed in black. The heat was on and the room felt warm as Maria entered it, but as soon as she saw the two men she felt cold, and she put on the jacket that she was carrying.

Maria had never seen her visitors before, and she asked them who they were. They told her they were with Dr. Black, her psychiatrist. She stared at their eyes, which weren't brown or blue, but a strange brownish grayish color. She found the experience frightening, and looked away.

The men asked her how she was and how she was doing at school, just a normal, polite conversation. As they talked Maria noticed several other strange things about her visitors. They looked the same, as if they were identical twins, their skin was smooth and featureless, no beard and no sign that they ever needed to shave at all.

Their hair was shiny black, each brushed in the same style and not a hair was out of place, their black suits, seemingly brand new, fitted perfectly as if tailor-made and having razor-sharp creases. Their ties and socks were also black, exactly the same black as their trousers and jackets.

One of the men then asked Maria if anything strange had happened at the convent recently. She instantly thought that they must mean what she had seen at the tennis court – but she was afraid to admit anything she knew to the strangers, so she said no.

The two men obviously knew she was lying as they continued to press the question. Just then the school lunchtime bell rang. The man asked what the bell was for and then told Maria she had better go to lunch, adding that they had to leave. Although the men looked to be like businessmen, they didn't appear to be wearing watches as one of them asked Maria the time.

The men had been drinking coffee during their talk with Maria, but when she shook hands with them as she was saying goodbye she noticed that their hands were ice cold, despite the fact that they had been holding hot cups of coffee during most of the conversation.

One of the men asked Sister Jennifer if Maria could show them the way out, saying finally that: "we'll be back to see you again."

She walked to the doorway and was amazed to see that the two men were walking and swinging their arms exactly in step with each other. They walked outside to their waiting black car and Maria noticed that although it was a windy day, their hair didn't move, as if it was glued down.

The car had a chauffeur, also dressed in black, who must have been waiting all this time. As the car moved off Maria noticed that the number plate had white characters on a black background, which she thought was strange. It also had mirrored windows so Maria couldn't see into the car, but she thought that the men could see out.

She caught a glimpse into the car when one of the men opened a door, but all she could see was black, no seats, and no dashboard. It was as if she was looking into a black hole.

The car moved off silently. There was no sound of an engine being started, no exhaust fumes. She was also mystified that although she saw the car turn out of the convent gate, she didn't see it moving up the hill that led to the convent. It had completely disappeared on the only road leading to the convent.

Maria stood where she was for several minutes, unable to move. She could hear Sister Jennifer calling to her, but she couldn't turn around and go to her. Sister Jennifer asked her if she was all right, at which point she "snapped out of it" and was able to move again. She asked Maria who the men were and Maria replied, saying that they were from Dr. Black; although they were both surprised that Dr. Black hadn't warned them that the men would be coming.

A few weeks later, when Maria saw Dr. Black, she asked her about her strange visitors. Dr. Black was shocked and informed Maria that she hadn't sent the men and would never send anyone without informing her first. Although Maria never saw her MIBs again, she did begin to develop psychic powers and have extraordinary experiences.

While still at the convent Maria: Bent a spoon, Uri Geller style – Timed herself swimming under water for five minutes before surfacing – She had an out-of-body experience - experienced an upsurge in her creative and academic abilities which was tested and verified by Dr. Black. Most amazingly of all, she also claimed that on one occasion, at night, she went out into the convent yard and began to fly. This was witnessed by several other girls, who ran around trying to catch her when she flew low enough.

After Maria left the convent her strange experiences and abilities continued. She found that she could make things disappear and reappear by just thinking about them. She could make light bulbs burn out; she started a stalled car engine (with a jammed starter motor and a totally dead battery) just by willing it. She claimed to be able to turn red traffic lights to green, repeatedly, even after they had just changed to red.

Maria Korn said the two men in black looked like identical twins. Their skin was smooth and featureless and their eyes were a strange brownish gray color. Her experience left her disoriented and frightened.

Strangely enough, Maria also experienced several episodes where she was unexpectedly teleported over the distance of several miles. Once, she stepped out of her front door to get the mail and found herself standing on the sidewalk in a neighborhood over five miles from her home. This happened without any warning and, as far as she could tell, was instantaneous.

Marie could offer no explanation on why these strange events centered on her. Although she is certain the UFO somehow exerted a weird type of mind control on her. Whatever happened to her, it was not a figment of her imagination. Many of the things that happened were witnessed by others. The UFO she saw left a depression and burn marks on the ground; her MIBs were seen by other people and they drank coffee that had been given to them; Maria's spoon bending, the increase in her academic and artistic abilities, light-bulb popping, some teleportation incidents, UFO sightings and other events can all be testified to.

STRANGE BEINGS THAT HAUNT AND HARASS

In another weird case, also in Great Britain, Mrs. Evans (pseudonym) of Portsmouth, Hampshire went to visit the local grocer's store one morning in the autumn of 1977. In the shop she saw a tall man, dressed in black. He was ahead of her, so she stood back to wait until he was served.

As she stood in line Mrs. Evans noticed that the man's gaze was fixed upon her. She found this unnerving; he looked at her as if he knew her, as if he had been expecting her. He left the store when it was her turn at the cash register.

When she left the shop, Mrs. Evans noticed that the man was standing nearby, as if waiting for someone. As she started to walk, he began walking also, keeping five or six paces ahead of her. As she watched him she began to form the impression that he was "unusual," although she couldn't say just why.

Mrs. Evans was half-way home when he turned left into a side road. As she crossed the road, she looked to her left out of curiosity only to see the same person standing in the middle of the road. Facing her now, their eyes met once more. He nodded three times, without any change in his facial expression. His gaze was intense and penetrating.

Then, to Mrs. Evans's utter amazement; he vanished without moving from the spot, "like someone turning out a light."

Thoroughly unnerved by now, she hurried home later recalling several strange things about the man: * His clothes looked brand new, as though they had only just been bought. He was dressed from head to foot in black (except for his white shirt). * His skin was albino-type white, as was his hair, which was wispy. His eyes were jet black, and he appeared to be in his early 50s, but there were no wrinkles on his skin, and no sign of any facial hair or stubble. *He had unusually broad shoulders, a narrow waist, and he walked upright with a stiff gait. There seemed to be no natural curve to his spine, which was seemingly perfectly straight.

This was not Mrs. Evans only encounter with the unusual; in 1979, over a year after her original MIB encounter. In her kitchen one day, she became aware that there was a figure standing beside her. Her husband walked in and shouted: "Who's that? What's he doing here?" Whereupon the figure, which did not seem to be totally solid, ran out of the open kitchen door and disappeared.

On another occasion, Mrs. Evans was returning home one evening when she saw, in the light from a street lamp, a tall figure. The figure was completely black and seemed to be wearing some kind of helmet, making her think of a scuba diver. At this moment her husband walked out of the front door and again shouted: "Who's that? What's he doing here?" He was convinced by now that this was Mrs. Evans's secret lover.

As her husband shouted, and as their dog started to bark, the figure glided forward, going through her neighbor's front garden hedge. She later recalled that the figure appeared at first to be completely solid and real, but it grew more transparent and eventually vanished as it slowly went through the bushes.

On another day, in broad daylight, Mrs. Evans encountered a "strange little man" who appeared in front of her and walked on by. On turning around, expecting to see his back, she was shocked to find that he had vanished.

She described the man as small, about five feet tall, olive skinned, large, round dark eyes, and black hair, slicked straight back. He seemed to be wearing some kind of RAF uniform except that it looked made-to-measure, perfectly cut and stitched. His shoes looked brand new but were not the current fashion. He walked towards her with his arms held up in front of him, gazing straight ahead with blank eyes.

On yet another occasion, again in daylight, Mrs. Evans was out walking, and she came upon a small van parked in the road. The van was white, with what looked like blue clouds and flowers painted on it. As she approached the van, its door suddenly opened and a little person jumped down in front of her. She just kept slowly walking as she and the little person gazed at each other.

At first she thought she was seeing a doll, or puppet wearing a checkered shirt and blue jeans, but she was startled as she looked into his eyes, which were jet black, marble-like, with two white dots where the pupils should have been. He seemed to have Eskimo features, with dull black, dead straight hair, roughly cut in a pageboy style. He seemed to have a knowing look in his eyes, which disturbed her.

As he passed by her she tried to look over her shoulder to see him, but her neck did not seem to be moving normally and she could only see him out of the corner of her eye. Mrs. Evans thought he seemed to be a freak of some kind, although he was perfectly proportioned.

In this case and others, it was the eyes that made her realize that she was not seeing something normal.

Another encounter came one evening in Mrs. Evans's front garden. She noticed movement within a large bush that was in the garden; as if a cat or other small animal was inside it. She remembers that everything seemed unnaturally still and quiet. Slowly, the bush began to part in two or three places. Instead of the cat that she was expecting, she was amazed to see faces, seemingly those of children.

When she realized that these were not children, she froze, and the hairs on the back of her neck stood up on end. She began to hear soft clucking sounds, the sort of noise one makes when trying to make friends with a shy animal. What she saw made her think of elves, pixies and the like. They did not seem to be totally solid looking and the bushes covered their lower bodies.

As their misshapen hands extended out towards her she decided that she had seen enough and ran indoors. As she ran upstairs her husband called out to her, asking if she had seen what it was that had just bolted out of the front garden. Later, with her heart still fluttering, she came down and looked nervously outside. The "elves" were gone, but she saw, walking towards her down the path near her home, a dark figure lit by an aura that moved with it. Before it suddenly disappeared, Mrs. Evans saw that the figure had short, dark curly hair and a pointy face with very high cheekbones. Its eyes seemed to glow as it stared at her in a menacing way.

Like others who have had similar experiences, Mrs. Evans found herself undergoing a whole series of unexplainable occurrences. As a young girl in 1947, there was a poltergeist in the family home, although she herself did not realize this and her parents who had never even heard of the poltergeist phenomenon did not tell her about it until many years later.

October 16, 1973 - her father sees a massive UFO. Winter 1977/Spring 1978 – Mrs. Evans sees (with her husband) her first UFO. Christmas 1978 - early New Years 1979 - UFOs, hauntings, poltergeists. Her husband and neighbors also experience these phenomena, but her house seems to be the focus. She begins to notice strange marks, burns, bruises, and puncture marks on her skin, which seem to appear in the mornings after restless nights.

Mrs. Evans reports seeing "about a dozen" UFOs from Christmas 1978 to November 1979. A blood-like substance appeared "out of thin air" at her home, also a "transparent, jelly-like" substance. Strong smells – she, her husband and her neighbor saw a small, yellowish cloud, accompanied by a strong smell of sulphur. On another occasion there was a strong, "overpowering" smell of incense, also smells of zoo animals' cages and wet animal fur.

On two occasions when "something unusual" passed over her head, she felt a click, or tap, on her temples, somewhat like a tiny electric shock to her brain. Things appeared and disappeared in her home: keys, jewelry, eye glasses. Her purse rose from the table, flew through the air and landed in her left hand. The teakettle whistled as if boiling, but there was no water in it, and the gas was not turned on. Flames came out of her fingernails, which turned bright turquoise overnight, the color being on the underside of the nail.

A "paper tape streamer" appeared out of nowhere and flew through the air in her living room. It bore the words: "Don't be afraid - we are coming back in

October." Her milkman saw her standing at her front door and waved to her, and then he turned around and saw her walking down the street towards him. Other people reported seeing her at various other places when she was actually miles away.

WHAT IS YOUR NUMBER?

In an article titled: "MIB Activity Reported From Victoria B.C.", (*Flying Saucer Review*, January 1982) Dr. P.M.H. Edwards, formerly professor of linguistics at the University of Victoria, detailed an unusual case of MIB teleportation.

In October 1981, three days after a UFO sighting in Victoria, British Columbia, Grant Breiland saw two sun-tanned expressionless men who lacked fingernails observing him at a K-Mart department store. They were stiff, seemingly "at attention," and were dressed in very dark blue clothes. They approached, and one asked Breiland in a monotonous, mechanical voice, "What is your name?" Their lips did not move when they spoke.

Breiland said, "I'm not going to tell you that." The other man asked where Breiland lived, and then, "What is your number?"

Breiland did not respond. The two strange men stared at him for a few seconds, then turned and left, but Breiland followed them out of curiosity.

The two men waited at the edge of a muddy, plowed field and, as Breiland watched them, he thought he heard someone call his name. Turning around, he saw no one. The two men walked into the field, and again, Breiland thought that he heard someone call out his name. Suddenly, the two men vanished three-quarters of the way across the field.

Checking around, Breiland was unable to locate any footprints in the muddy field. It was as if the two men were ghosts. Breiland noted that, mysteriously, no other persons were in sight at the busy shopping area during the entire incident, and the setting was only repopulated after the strange men had vanished. The "depopulation" anomaly has been noted in other UFO and MIB cases, and has been termed the "Oz effect" by British UFO researcher Jenny Randles. This zone of unreality seems to indicate that these incidents could be paranormal in nature.

PROJECT ALIEN MIND CONTROL -- UFO REVIEW SPECIAL

COMMENTS FROM MUSICIAN TOM DELONGE OF BLINK-182

You've had your phone tapped?

Yeah, yeah, I did. For quite some time. Years ago, there was somebody who was gathering 150 hours of top secret testimony specifically for Congressional hearings on government projects and the U.S. secret space program. People from NASA, Rome, the Vatican, you name it, they're all on there. The top 36 hours that summarized the best parts of all of that footage, I had it hidden in my house for a period of time, and, during that time, I was flying this person out along with somebody that was Wernher von Braun's right-hand assistant. Wernher von Braun was a Nazi scientist that we brought over to build our Apollo rockets that got us to the moon, and on his deathbed he told this person a bunch of stuff, and I was flying them out to Los Angeles and we were taking certain meetings. At that time a lot of weird stuff started happening.

Were you concerned about your safety at all?

Partially. Because they do weird stuff. At the time I didn't know it, but the person I was dealing with was being awoken in the middle of the night with clicking and buzzing noises and falling on the ground vomiting, every morning at 4 a.m. I know now that those are artifacts from mind-control experiments, where the same technology that we use to find oil underground, we can zap somebody at the same frequency that the brain operates on, and it can cause some really horrific things to happen. But I didn't know this until 10 years later. I got caught in the middle of it, and this was the time when I was on the cover of *"Rolling Stone,"* so I think these guys, whoever was running this operation, were like, "What the fuck? How did this kid show up?"

QUOTES FROM PAPERMAG.COM

John F. Kennedy sent a memo to the head of the CIA seeking documents about UFOs just 10 days before he was assassinated. Were his killers part of a "Manchurian Candidate" assassination squad?

PROJECT ALIEN MIND CONTROL -- UFO REVIEW SPECIAL

PROJECT ALIEN MIND CONTROL -- UFO REVIEW SPECIAL

THE idea of mind control by the government or clandestine groups is in itself a disturbing concept. Yet the possibility that humans are being mentally and spiritually manipulated by an ultra-terrestrial intelligence is a scenario far more horrifying to contemplate.

A number of investigators have suspected that UFOs may be responsible for somehow controlling the minds of some witnesses and abductees. UFO literature is filled with hundreds of cases in which observers have been subjected to continuous harassments following an encounter with a UFO. Some witnesses report strange, ghost-like phenomena in their homes. In other cases, weird, mechanical-sounding voices, purported to be "messages" from extraterrestrials, begin emanating from their phones, radios and televisions.

Some witnesses persist in believing that they are being harassed controlled day and night by UFO entities. Cases of UFO mind manipulation are actually quite common. Yet very little is known about it because of the scant research being conducted.

Investigators have attempted to distance themselves from cases of alien mind control. Most feel that the witnesses who complain of such attacks are probably mentally ill. However, the research that has been done shows that accounts of UFO mind control are almost always identical.

The pattern that emerges usually follows a close encounter with a UFO. The eyewitness goes through a period of anxiety, during which he is unable to consciously remember certain aspects of the incident. Within months, the personality of the observer actually changes. Eventually, it may change to the point where he finds it impossible to get along with co-workers, friends or even family. Personal tragedy seems to strike many of those who have had UFO experiences.

In some cases, the eyewitness discovers he has developed certain "gifts" or abilities. Though they may appear to be beneficial at first, too often this is not the case. Among these unusual abilities are powers of ESP, precognition, or psychokinesis. In addition, a heightened intelligence level or an unusual increase in physical strength may be noticed. Such peculiarities will often manifest themselves shortly before a person is about to be controlled. Shortly after this, he may begin slipping into a "trance," during which time it appears as if an alien intelligence has "taken over" his body and is using his brain. There are hundreds of so-called "mental contactees" who claim to receive information and data of a highly advanced scientific and philosophical nature.

During the 1950's and 60's, this method of communicating with UFO occupants (better known as channeling) became so popular that entities calling themselves "Ashtar," "Agar," and "Monka" were heard from daily, somewhere in the world.

There is no doubt that this phenomenon is widespread and it is by no means limited to the United States. Cases of mind-altering UFOs seem to be occurring at an alarming rate. There have been reports of entire communities being placed under a strange "spell," with the simultaneous appearance of UFOs in the area.

MENTAL INVADERS

A large-scale attempt to invade and seize the minds of human beings occurred on April 29, 1967, when a coastal village on the outskirts of Rio de Janeiro became the target of a mysterious malady that may have been perpetrated by a strange craft sighted overhead.

In an hour's time, the citizens of Barra de Tijuca, Brazil were literally forced into establishing contact with an unearthly intelligence, which quickly subdued many people in the town. The series of disturbing events began at noon, when an emergency telephone call reached Dr. Jeronemo Rodrigues Morales, chief physician at Barr de Tijuca's general hospital. An excited voice explained how a man in his late 60s had fallen unconscious on the beach near town.

Dr. Morales immediately drove to the scene. Upon arriving he found the man brushing sand from his clothes and talking to a crowd of people who had gathered to offer help. "I was merely walking about the sand dunes," the man explained. "I had been watching the gulls high above the water, when suddenly I blacked out."

An examination ruled out the possibility of a heart attack and Dr. Morales decided that the man had suffered a mild case of sunstroke. Within minutes, another call came in with the news that a fisherman had been discovered in shallow water beneath a nearby bridge, and was said to be trembling from shock.

Dr. Morales quickly drove to the area and arrived just in time to see the "stricken" fisherman casually drying himself off, and asking what all the excitement was about.

When the doctor explained that he had blacked out, the man seemed insulted. "I'm not sick," he argued. "I feel perfectly well." He assured Dr. Morales that he had been tossing his nets into these waters every day for twenty years without any difficulty, and would do so for twenty more.

Within a short while, Dr. Morales received word of six other "stricken" individuals. All followed the identical pattern: People keeling over and then reviving themselves without aid, and, after a flurry of excitement, insisting that nothing was wrong.

While Dr. Morales was treating a mother and her young son, both who had collapsed together on the beach, he noticed something high overhead. Glistening in the sun, the doctor observed an enormous disc-shaped UFO over the town. The craft was darting about in the sky at tremendous speeds. Several other physicians and nurses on the hospital staff reported that they had seen the UFO suspended over the town since noon. Shortly after that, the object disappeared along with the strange illness. Still, the town's people had not heard the last from their strange visitor.

Three days later, another UFO, similar to the first, appeared over the city. Once more, a number of people dropped unconscious to the ground. During these two days, many other individuals were treated at the hospital for headaches and dizziness. Some even reported hearing strange voices talking to them in an unknown language.

VOICES FROM THE SKY

In the weeks after the strange incident at Barra de Tijuca, people who had experienced the mysterious malady began to speak openly about what happened to them. Most reported a strange voice in their head that spoke in a guttural language no one understood. Others said the voice was clearly understandable and kept repeating the phrase "do not be afraid" over and over. One man said the voice told him not to tell anyone what had happened to him, and promised that it would return soon. What has not been reported are the continuing strange incidents that have plagued many of the town's people of Barra de Tijuca in the years after their initial event.

One Brazilian UFO investigator wrote that: "The people of Barra de Tijuca continue to be haunted by the insistent voices in their heads. Most will no longer talk to outsiders about their problems. Those that do tell frighteningly similar stories of voices that control every aspect of their daily lives. The voices, the towns people say, originate from alien beings hovering high overhead in their UFOs."

While some people say that they have learned to "tune out" the constant chatter in their heads, others have not been so fortunate. The suicide rate in town is staggering. Some try to drown out the voices with drugs or alcohol. Others try and leave Barra de Tijuca for good. Nothing really seems to work against the continuing torment.

Strangely enough, when asked what the voices talk about, most town people say they can't remember, that the voices didn't want them to remember. Could there be other towns across the globe experiencing the same harassment? Are the inhabitants of these towns being prepared through mind control for some kind of unknown situation or mission in the future? Might we be faced someday with an army of hypnotically controlled humans, ready through years of mental manipulation, to do the bidding of their otherworldly controllers?

In his book **Passport to Magonia**, Jacques Vallee writes of a chilling account of possible alien mind control in the former Soviet Union. "In 1971, an eminent scientist in the field of plasma research, died under suspicious circumstances, he was murdered by a mentally disturbed woman who pushed him into the path of a train at the Moscow subway station. The accused women claimed that a 'voice' from space had instructed her to kill this particular man, and she felt unable to resist the order."

Vallee has also stated that he has heard from "trustworthy sources" that Russian police are disturbed about the recent increase in cases of this nature. "Quite often," Vallee maintains, "Mentally unstable people are known to run wildly across a street, protesting they are being pursued by Martians, but the present wave of mental troubles is an aspect of the UFO problem that deserves special attention."

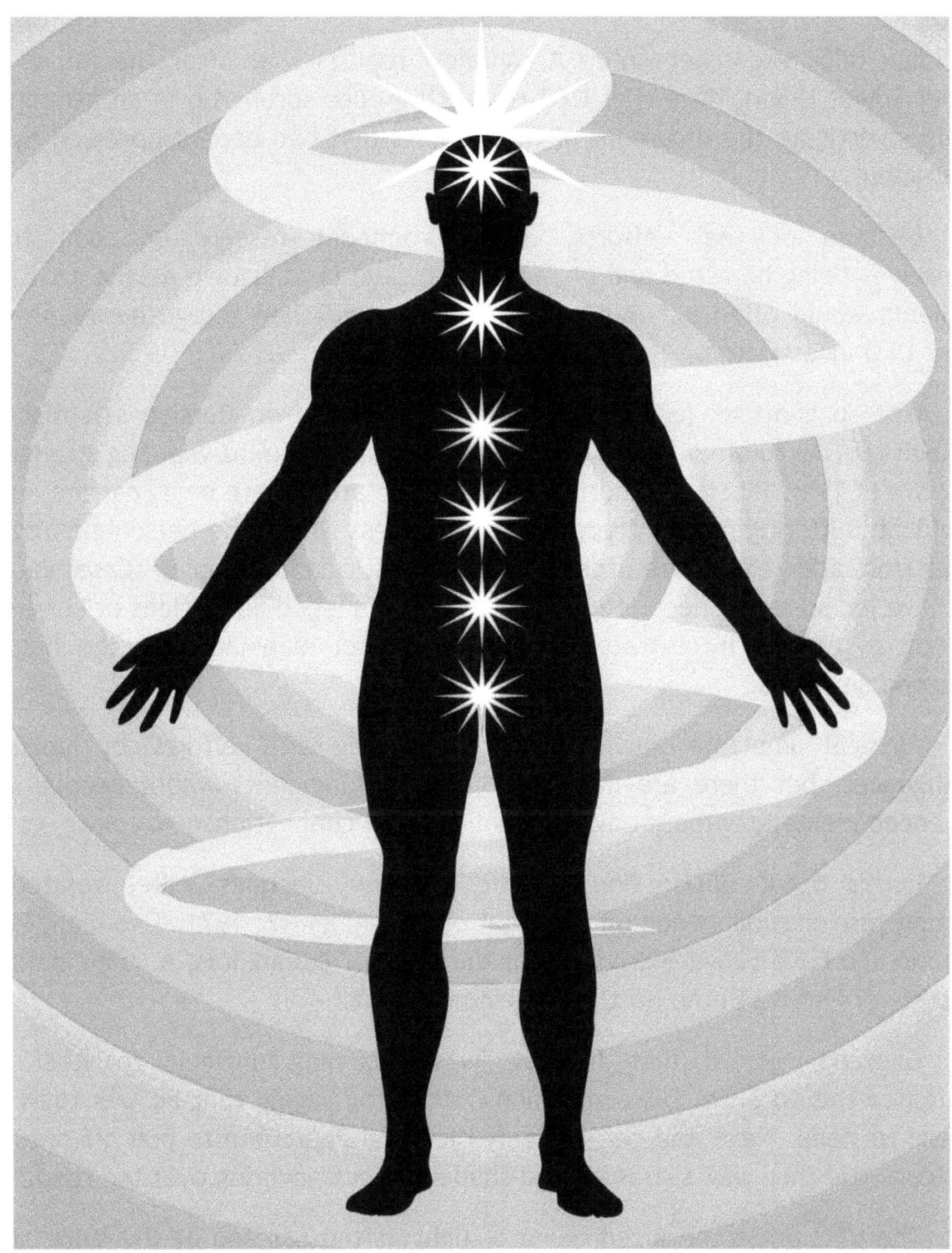

UFO encounters sometimes have an undeniable physical component. However, it is clear that they frequently involve paranormal phenomena as well. They are sometimes similar to dream/trance states and ghostly experiences, and can be highly surreal.

Ukrainian UFO researcher Anton A. Anfalow reports that after the fall of the former Soviet Union, dozens of UFO research groups sprung up in an attempt to finally investigate the thousands of UFO reports that had been suppressed by the government.

Because of their efforts, many prominent researchers soon found themselves being harassed and physically attacked by unknown assailants. These assailants would often act like muggers, but would then forego easier prey to target UFO investigators.

One such attack led to the murder of well-known Russian scientist and UFOlogist Dr. A. Zolotov. Dr. Zolotov was attacked by a knife-wielding stranger in the town of Tver. Russian authorities say that the attacks are being carried out by individuals suffering from a "type of mental illness where the person claims that voices from alien beings are ordering them to kill certain people." Cases such as this have led some to speculate that the wave of alleged abductions of humans is part of an agenda by extraterrestrials to control mankind with the help of electronic implants.

Physical implants may be used for long-term efforts by unknown intelligences, but there are many reported UFO incidents where people were influenced mentally without any apparent physical connection.

In his book, **UFOs: The Psychic Solution**, Jacques Vallee related an amazing case that happened on the night of November 17, 1971. Two men, Paulo Gaetano and Elvio B. were driving near the town of Bananeiras, a municipality in the state of Paraíba in the Northeast Region of Brazil.

Gaetano noticed that the car was becoming difficult to steer and mentioned this to Elvio. His companion reacted by saying that he was tired and wanted to sleep. Next, the car suddenly died and Paulo had to pull off onto the shoulder. He then saw a strange, egg-shaped object hovering over the road.

The UFO projected a red beam of light at the car and at the same time, several small beings materialized and took Gaetano out of the stalled car. The man was taken into the craft and placed onto a small table. After tying down his arms, the entities lowered down a device that looked like an x-ray machine. With this device, the beings collected blood from a cut near his elbow.

Next, Gaetano was shown two pictures; one was a map of the town of Itaperuna, the other was a photograph of an atomic explosion. At this point, Gaetano doesn't remember what happened or how he got back to the car. He did tell investigators later that he remembered being helped by Elvio, but did not recall how they got home.

Elvio's story on what happened that night is very different. He said that near Bananeiras, Gaetano had begun to act nervous, saying there was a flying saucer following them. Elvio didn't see any UFO behind them, there was only a bus. Elvio added that the car had slowed down and stopped, and that Gaetano had gotten out and collapsed behind the car, with the door on the driver's side remaining open.

Elvio managed to get Gaetano on his feet and boarded the bus that had been behind them. The pair went to the town of Itaperuna, where Gaetano was examined by the first-aid station. The police went to the site and found the car still on the side of the road. Elvio could not explain what had happened to Gaetano and why the car door was open. He did not remember when Gaetano had got out, and could not explain why they had left the car behind and taken the bus. The police found no trace on the car that could explain the wound on Paulo's arm.

Vallee comments that some experiments with microwaves suggest it is becoming technically feasible for sensory impressions to be projected into people's minds at a distance. He asks: "Is this part of the technology that is involved in the UFO phenomenon? Are we dealing with a technology that systematically confuses the witnesses?"

Another possibility is that instead of being influenced by some kind of advanced mind-control devices acting on the physical brain, the mind could be influenced on the astral level without the use of any physical technology. Many UFO abductions do seem to have a physical component. There is certainly a great deal of evidence that UFOs can manifest physically and leave physical traces. In some cases people may have been physically taken on board these vehicles, and there are a few abduction cases in which the abducteé was apparently dropped off miles from the pickup point.

If humans are occasionally taken on board materialized craft, then a physical medical examination is not inconceivable, though it may only be a simulated one, conducted by paranormal entities rather than by extraterrestrial scientists. However, many aspects of abduction experiences sound like visions or dreams.

Abduction cases with definite physical elements seem to be rare compared with the numerous cases where there is no hard evidence of anything extraordinary. Many aspects of abduction experiences sound like visions or dreams. In these cases the entire experience could be taking place on the mental plane, and reflect a variety of influences. Some of these cases could be generated during the hypnosis session itself, while others may originate in an actual unusual experience.

UFO encounters may actually take place on several different levels...a physical level, a mental level and an astral or spiritual level. Whatever the source is for the intelligence behind the UFO phenomena, it apparently can operate in ways that is completely outside of the realm of known science. This is why many religious leaders over the years have warned about avoiding any contact with UFO intelligences. The fact that these unknown entities can influence people on a spiritual level is frightening and is reminiscent of the ancient mythologies of demons and other malevolent spirits.

ALIEN IMPLANTS

In recent years, hundreds of people claiming to have had contact with aliens also believe they have been implanted with strange electronic devices. The exact purpose of these microchip-like implants, reportedly found embedded in the skin of abductees, remains unknown. Until recently their existence has only been supported by anecdotal evidence. However, as the abduction phenomenon gathers momentum, more physical evidence is being gathered and studied by doctors and scientists.

According to UFO folklore, implants are usually located in the nasal cavity. In some famous cases, such as the alleged abduction of author Whitley Streiber, brain scans have shown disturbances in an area of the brain close to that part of the body.

Some abductees have reported experiencing nose bleeds, believing that implants were forced into their nostrils so that their brains could be monitored and controlled.

In recent years, however, implants have begun appearing in different parts of the body, sometimes in the back of the neck, behind an ear or in the hands and feet. Hard evidence of purported alien technology has been very hard to come by. On August 19, 1995, Ventura, California surgeon Dr. Roger Leir and his surgical team, along with Houston alien contact investigator and Certified Hypnotherapist Derrel Sims, removed three "implants" from two people, a man and a woman who had experienced what they believed to be UFO related incidents in their life.

Two of the implants were removed from the woman's toes. The third was in the back of the man's hand. All three were attached to nerves where no nerves are known to exist. So far, two additional surgeries have been performed. Three out of four patients turned out to have nearly identical, highly anomalous iron alloy objects involved.

In all cases, ultra hard metallic highly magnetic "cores" were surrounded by an ultra-dense dark gray membrane which couldn't be cut with a brand-new scalpel. The membrane somehow prevented any sign of inflammation or rejection. Dr. Leir noted that: "If the implants can teach us how to prevent tissue rejection, we could revolutionize surgery."

Interestingly, the membranes on these objects turned out to be made of a tough matrix of proteins from skin and blood. This could explain why the body accepted the objects so readily. It might also explain the very common "scoop marks" that abductees often find on their bodies.

The removed tissue could be wrapped around an implant to "fool" the body into believing the object is part of the system. Also not so easily explained is how the implants got into these people's bodies. Even with a powerful magnifying glass, Dr. Leir could find no sign of a scar or other evidence of a point of entry for objects which had come to be placed deep in the victims tissues.

If implants are actually electronic devices of some kind...what is their purpose? The most prevalent explanation for implants is that they are used to tag an individual to make sure they can be found again. Others believe that the implants are bugging devices, used to monitor conversations and actions. Another theory is that the implants are a means of mentally controlling human subjects.

Often, victims of UFO abduction complain of the feeling that their minds are being influenced by aliens. Abductees report a number of experiences that could be induced by the implants: Buzzing, beeping and strange voices, missing time, inexplicable emotions in inappropriate circumstances, loss of self control and telepathic communication. Many report the disturbance of electrical objects in their presence, perhaps a side effect of such implant technologies.

THE PURPOSE OF IMPLANTS

One certain group who refers to themselves as "The Light," stated in an e-mail received by the author that people worldwide have been implanted with devices to allow certain kinds of control by extraterrestrial entities.

"Extraterrestrials are currently living among us as humans to monitor human development and assist mankind. Through metabolism cloning, they have the capability to transform their body into a human form taking several minutes. By choosing a desired path, they discreetly & consciously live under a human guise among people without revealing their identity until the correct time. Before society can accept the alien presence, its culture and organization must be changed, which is why they form an influential global network responsible for waves of UFO and alien phenomenon. These part alien/part-human individuals or hybrid-aliens are called 'Guardians.' The Guardians have been selectively breed with humans over the millenniums in order to produce spiritually evolved beings.

"Alien races have visited the earth for thousands of years for different purposes, but the explanation behind the majority of abductions is that alien beings based on earth are implementing a program to implant selected individuals with technically advanced information to condition, educate, and improve humanity. Across the globe and after an examination period, these people were chosen because of specific traits these beings were comfortable with. This microscopic implant, which lies dormant, is inserted into the brain through a condensed light source or manually using surgical instruments.

"The implant contains the foundation for understanding basic extraterrestrial knowledge, principles, and concepts. Very simple examples include: cures for diseases, undiscovered power sources, formulas for food processing and growing, applications of light, utilization of crystals, etc. The power of advanced knowledge will become second nature without ever affecting the implantees personality and memory. The process of learning has been condensed in a microscopic implant: all the chosen will have a sudden interest in an area that they never had previously as if an extraterrestrial course has been studied. This knowledge will be permanent, even if the implant is surgically removed. There are parts of the human brain that naturally becomes a 'biological storage area' for the information stored in the implants.

"A guide is free to scan any field of interest he or she desires. After implantation, these people are called 'Implantees.' After the implant is unlocked, these individuals are called 'Guides.' The Formation is the global event that will simultaneously notify and gather the selected implantees and activate or unlock the implants. The crucial conditioning period after The Formation is called 'The Convergence.'

"The implant also acts as a tracking device in order for the movements of each implantee to be occasionally monitored by a Guardian in close proximity. Through this means, each person will be protected and prevented from an unnatural death. Prior to The Formation, each implantee, regardless of what he or she is doing, will be confronted and informed in detail by a Guardian either verbally or telepathically of what is about to take place. Simultaneously across the world in different countries, all implantees will be transported by means of small crafts to larger crafts situated above the earth. Here the implantee is free to mingle and converse with others across the globe that has been selected, which may or may not include past acquaintances.

"Demonstrations will be given, there will be freedom to interact with hybrid-aliens, and virtually all questions will be answered. Sometime during this period, the implant will be activated or 'unlocked' via a harmless fine-tuning light directed at each person's head, leaving a small red mark for several days. The Convergence has now commenced...the great transformation and advancement these extraterrestrials have been guiding humanity toward. The Guides are now ready to introduce revolutionary and innovative ideas to mankind. For the first time in history, there will be a direct relationship between alien knowledge and society."

CONTACTEES - OR ALIEN MIND CONTROL VICTIMS?

The UFO phenomenon is complex and offers no easy answers. On one side UFOs appear to be physical, constructed machines, flown by creatures who claim to be from other planets. On the other side is the unphysical nature of the phenomena, with

UFOs and the strange beings associated with them manifesting like ghosts. People who are unlucky enough to get caught up in the confusing world of UFOs and their occupants are often subjected to weird forms of possession, behavioral changes and mind control. Victims of UFO abduction usually report periods of "missing time" which is almost certainly achieved with some kind of mental manipulation of the abductee.

The late John Keel speculated that the contactee syndrome is a fundamental reprogramming process. No matter what frame of reference is being used, the experience usually begins with either the sudden flash of light or a sound - a humming, buzzing or beeping. The subject's attention is riveted to a pulsing, flickering light of dazzling intensity. He finds he is unable to move a muscle and is rooted to the spot.

Next the flickering light goes through a series of color changes and a seemingly physical object begins to take form. The light diminishes revealing a UFO, or an entity of some sort. What is really happening is that the percipient is first entranced by the flickering light. From the moment he feels paralyzed, he loses touch with reality and begins to hallucinate. The light remains a light, but the contactees mind is hypnotized to see a spaceship and/or a strange alien creature.

Keel writes in his book, **The Mothman Prophecies**, that he was concerned with the falsified memories of the contactees. "I wondered what happened to the bodies of these people while their minds were taking trips in flying saucers. Trips that often lasted for hours, even for days."

A young college professor in New York State was haunted by the same question in 1967. After investigating a UFO-related poltergeist case, he suffered possession and was led to believe that he had committed a daring jewel robbery while he was in a trance or possessed state. He abandoned Ufology and nearly suffered a total nervous breakdown in the aftermath.

Are contactees and abduction victims being used by exterior intelligence's to carry out crimes, even murder? The answer is a disturbing yes. If you review the history of political assassinations you will find that many were performed by so-called religious fanatics who were obeying the "voice of God," or were in an obvious state of possession when they committed their crime. Assassins such as Sirhan Sirhan, who murdered Robert Kennedy, had a strange fascination with the occult and hypnosis. It is not unusual for them to say that they have no recollection of committing the crime...a telltale indication of mind control.

In contactee parlance, persons who perform involuntary acts are said to be "used." A contactee may feel a sudden impulse to go for a pointless late-night walk or drive. During that drive he encounters, he thinks, the space people and is abducted. Actually his body goes on to, say, Point A where he picks up a letter or object left there by another contactee. He carries the letter or object to Point B and deposits it. Later he has no memories of these actions.

ALIEN ABDUCTIONS OR MILITARY EXPERIMENTS?

According to Helmut Lammer Ph.D., UFO abductions are generally a very complex phenomena. For skeptics, journalists and the public, it is difficult to believe that abductions by alien beings have their basis in physical reality. However, well respected researchers have shown that the core of the UFO abduction phenomenon cannot be explained psychologically as hallucinations or mass delusions. Recently, some UFO abductees have reported that they have also been kidnapped by military intelligence personnel and taken to hospitals and/or military facilities, some of which are described as being underground.

Very few books on the subject of UFO abductions have mentioned these experiences. Especially disconcerting is the fact that abductees recall seeing military intelligence personnel together with alien beings, working side by side in these secret facilities. Researchers in the field of mind control suggest that these cases are evidence that the whole UFO abduction phenomenon is staged by the intelligence community as a cover for their illegal experiments. Could the whole abduction scenario be a carefully manipulated hypnotic cover for experimentation by government or military intelligence services?

The alleged military involvement in the abduction phenomenon could be evidence that the military uses abductees for mind control experiments as test-targets for microwave weapons. Moreover, the military could be monitoring and even kidnapping abductees for information gathering purposes during, before and after a UFO abduction.

Lammer's research suggests that abductees are often harassed by dark, unmarked helicopters that fly around their houses. The mysterious helicopter activity goes back to the late sixties and early seventies, when they showed an apparent interest in animal mutilations, but not in alleged UFO abductees. However, UFO researcher Raymond E. Fowler reported some helicopter activity in connection with UFO witnesses during the seventies.

Many abductees report interaction with military intelligence personnel after the helicopters begin to appear. Debbie Jordan reports, for instance, in a side note of her book Abducted!, while she was with a friend, she was kidnapped, drugged and taken to a kind of military hospital where she was examined by a medical doctor. This doctor told her he was going to remove a "bug" from her ear and proceeded to take out an implant that resembled a BB.

The abduction experiences of Leah Haley and Katharina Wilson also includes military-type encounters. Some of Wilson's experiences are reminiscent of reported mind control experiments. For example, she writes of a flashback from her childhood where she remembers being forced into what appeared to be a Skinner Box that may have been used for behavior modification purposes. In some military abduction cases military doctors searched for implants and sometimes even implanted the abductee with what appeared to be a man-made implant.

The technology does exist for small, radio frequency electronic implants. More than three million animals worldwide have been successfully implanted with a transponder manufactured by Destron-Fearing. The transponder is a passive radio frequency identification tag, designed to work in conjunction with a compatible radio-frequency ID reading system.

PROJECT ALIEN MIND CONTROL -- UFO REVIEW SPECIAL

The transponder is activated by a low-frequency radio signal. It then transmits the ID code to the reading system. The smallest transponder is about the size of an uncooked grain of rice. The transponder's tiny electronic circuit is energized by the low-power radio beam sent by a compatible reading device.

A similar bio-chip for humans was patented in 1989 by Dr. Daniel Man. The homing device, which can be implanted under the skin, was originally developed to locate missing children. This device is slightly larger than the Destron implant and a small surgical incision must be made for it to be implanted. Dr. Man claims that the best location for his implant may be behind the ear.

It is possible that some of the information received from abductees may be cover stories, induced by hypno-programming techniques of military psychiatrists. It is also possible that the military uses rubber alien masks and special effects during a supposed alien abduction. Katharina Wilson reported flashbacks where she remembered holding a rubber mask of an alien head in her hands. Facts such as these lead some mind control researchers to believe that all alien abductees are actually mind control and/or genetic experiments staged by a secret group within the government of the United States.

In a declassified memo dated February 17, 1994, former Naval Intelligence Commander Scott Jones, Ph.D. wrote to White House Presidential Science Advisor John Gibbons: "Whatever Roswell turns out to be, it is only the opening round. I urge you to take another look at the *UFO Matrix of Belief* that I provided you last year. My mention of mind-control technology at the February 4 meeting was quite deliberate. Please be careful about this. There are reasons to believe that some governmental group has interwoven research about this [mind-control] technology with alleged UFO phenomena. If that is correct, you can expect to run into early resistance when inquiring about UFOs, not because of the UFO subject, but because that has been used to cloak research and applications of mind-control activity."

PROJECT ALIEN MIND CONTROL -- UFO REVIEW SPECIAL

Above: Albert K. Bender and his solo MIB. Bender, who died in 2016, gave up his interest in UFOs after being threatened by the Men in Black.

Below: The late Jack Robinson, whose apartment building was stalked by a MIB, is seen here in Manhattan with Gray Barker, whose book *They Knew Too Much About Flying Saucers* was the first best seller on the subject in 1956.

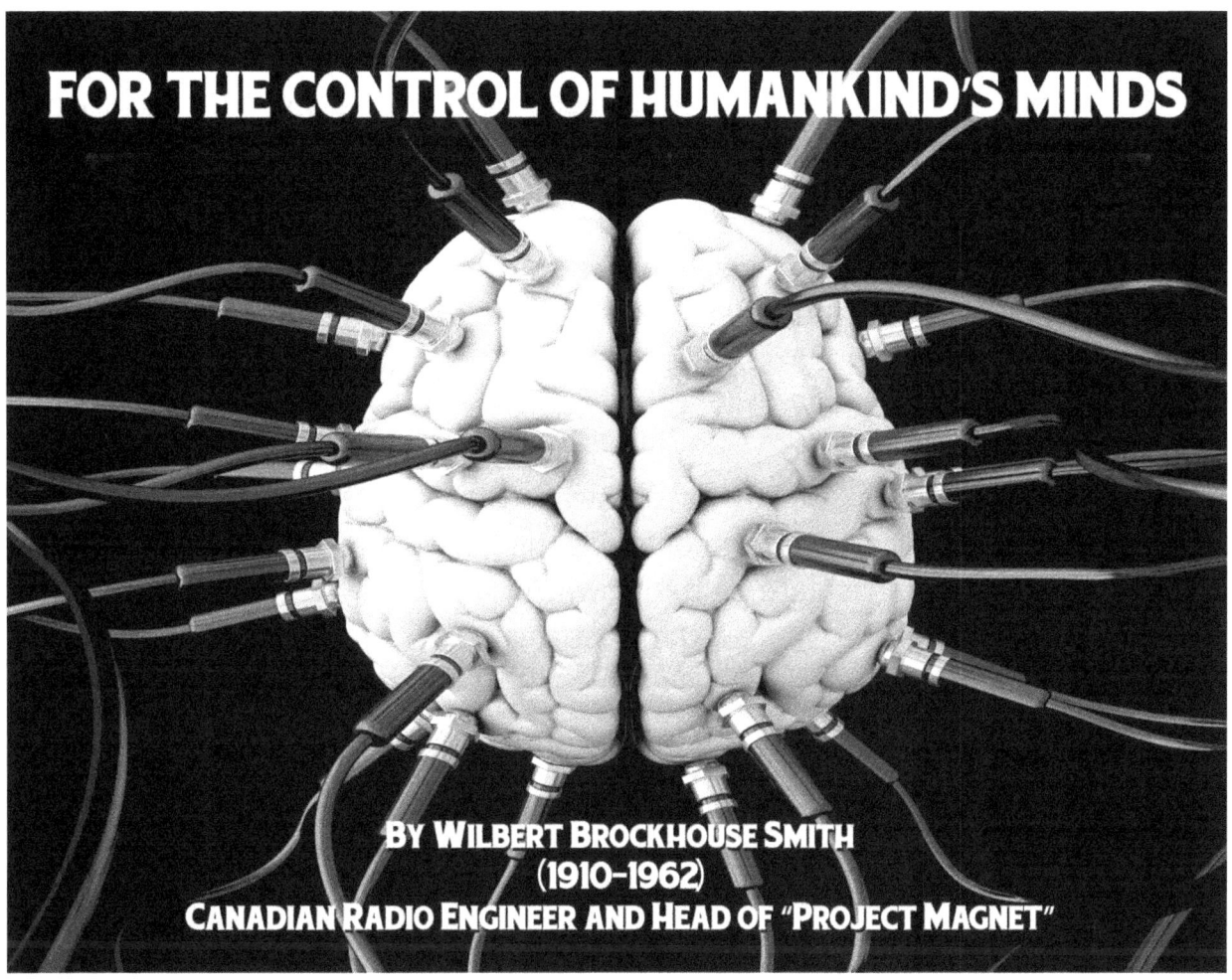

I propose to give the reader a warning of a grave nature which we are all, consciously or unconsciously, facing in a world in which two great forces are striving to gain control of man's mind. This struggle has been going on from time immemorial, but never in the world's history has the conflict been more intense than it is in this present era of confusion and unrest. In the old days, mankind was often made to suffer physically unspeakable things in the name of power, but today, with man's mind more developed and better educated, he is now facing the prospect of a refinement of even greater mental and spiritual cruelty – unless he is prepared to correct himself with right thinking.

The two great forces involved in trying to influence man's thinking may be described as POSITIVE, i.e., thoughts in harmony with the concept of a love of God and the brotherhood of man, and NEGATIVE, those encompassing anti-Christ motives designed to gain control over man for the purpose of power. This battle for man's mind is being waged on two fronts, the physical and the metaphysical, and the object of the fight is to bring about either the spiritual salvation or destruction of Homo sapiens.

To deal first with the physical aspects, no matter how hard we may all strive to be strong-minded and individualistic, we are all subtly influenced by the spoken and written word and other forms of thought communication, particularly through the mediums of books, newspapers, radio and television. In the latter field, as the sponsors know only too well, even the "commercials" play an important role in making up our minds to purchase certain products. In our business and social lives, we are often swayed by the thoughts of others, and some people, too apathetic to form opinions themselves, are willing to accept the views of others more articulate as their own. In all our daily contacts, a little of the good, bad or indifferent, as the case may be, is rubbing off on us and influencing our thinking.

These then are some of the factors we are facing in the battle for man's mind on the physical plane. But what of the metaphysical influences at work on us – the invisible but all-powerful forces on the purely mental plane? Whether we realize it or not, we are equally susceptible, if not more so, at the subconscious level to these more subtle influences. Man's brain, which in reality operates on the metaphysical plane, is like a two-way radio which transmits and receives messages along the airwaves of the universe – and his receiving mechanism is open to thoughts both good and bad, which he either accepts or rejects according to his stage of evolution.

Most of us are well aware of the truth of mental telepathy and many of us have had personal experiences of thought communication between loved ones often thousands of miles away. But what of special thoughts being beamed at us deliberately for a specific purpose, at both the conscious and unconscious levels, from another plane of existence?

Messages received through esoteric sources, purporting to come from Space Brothers who take an active interest in the spiritual welfare of the inhabitants of our planet, warn us that an even greater conflict is being fought on the metaphysical plane where intelligent beings of both a higher and a lower spiritual order than ourselves are waging a fierce battle for man's mind. The lower or negative forces, damned themselves by wrong thinking, are projecting strong thoughts Earthward in an attempt to bring about our spiritual downfall. On the other hand, Space Brothers and other spiritual guardians of our planet are concentrating equally hard on sending out positive thoughts of goodwill and brotherly love. Thus we are being bombarded from the metaphysical plane by two conflicting schools of thought, and, free will being the criterion of spiritual advancement, it is left to us which we choose to accept. However, from a purely logical point of view, if we want to save ourselves a lot of sorrow – both in this life and lives to come – we should arm ourselves mentally against the onslaught of negative thoughts.

This is no time for confused or apathetic thinking, which are often the breeding ground of negative thoughts. Nor should we be just receivers and disseminators of the thoughts we pick up. Rather, we should get on the transmitting end and constantly project positive thoughts of goodwill to all. Every positive thought neutralizes a negative thought, so we shall be serving not only ourselves but all humanity.

In the final analysis, there are two simple, clear-cut maxims to be observed for complete protection from the negative forces at work on this planet: (1) Acknowledgment and love of God as Father of all Creation, and (2) brotherly love extended to ALL his creatures throughout the universe. Anything else which interferes with these two beliefs should be vigorously rejected. Further, if we return love for hate, hate will die of malnutrition, for it can only feed on returned hatred. Let us rather pray for spiritual enlightenment for these wretched souls who seek to harm us.

In conclusion, if any of you have doubts about the veracity of the telepathic and inspirational messages received from Space Brothers and others interested in the welfare of our planet, just ask yourselves this one vital question – "Are these messages good and true and for the benefit of mankind on Earth?" If, as you surely must, you come up with an answer of "Yes," then it is obvious that it is the hand of God at work, no matter what medium He chooses to use.

We can perhaps take comfort from the fact that the odds against ANYONE surviving a nuclear war are so great that it is very unlikely that either side will be the first to "press the button," and maybe it is for this reason that the Russians are turning to a more subtle weapon – the manipulation of man's mind. Their success with the Pavlov experiments and the subsequent brainwashing techniques led them to go a step further – the establishment of an extensive psychical research program with the main emphasis on mental telepathy and ESP. How far they have gone with this program, we do not know, but one well-known American columnist found it necessary to warn the U.S. government that the newly-developed Russian technique of "cloud busting" (an expression used to describe the production of physical effects by intense mental concentration) would bear their close investigation. The Soviets apparently realize the potentialities of the power of thought far better than we do, and we must remember that power of any kind can be used for either good or evil.

There are those who are much more easily manipulated once they have experienced a UFO encounter.

PROJECT ALIEN MIND CONTROL -- UFO REVIEW SPECIAL

OUR CONTRIBUTORS

Photos and Brief Tidbits About the Writers

SEAN CASTEEL

Veteran researcher of UFOs, alien abductions and author/co-author of *"UFOs, Prophecy and the End of Time," "The Heretic's UFO Guidebook," "The Search for the Pale Prophet in Ancient America,"* and *"Behind the Flying Saucers: The Truth About the Aztec UFO Crash."* Sean's work has been published in the U.K., Italy, Romania and Australia. He has been a regular contributor to "UFO Universe," "Fate" and "UFO Magazine."
http://www.amazon.com/Sean-Casteel/e/B018WOBVIK/ref=sr_ntt_srch_lnk_6?qid=1468343667&sr=1-6

TIM R. SWARTZ

A native of Indiana and Emmy-Award winning television producer, he is the editor of the online "Conspiracy Journal" and author of *"The Lost Journals of Nikola Tesla," "Men of Mystery, Nikola Tesla and Otis T. Carr," "Admiral Byrd's Journey Beyond the Poles," "Time Travel: Fact Not Fiction"* and *"Mind Stalkers."* He has appeared on the History Channel's "Ancient Aliens" and is cohost of "Exploring the Bizarre," broadcast over KCORradio.com.
www.conspiracyjournal.com

ADAM GORIGHTLY

For over two decades Adam Gorightly's articles have appeared in nearly every zine, underground magazine, counter-cultural publication, and conspiratorial website imaginable. Bringing a mischievous sense of Prankster-Discordianism to the zany world of fringe culture, once Gorightly connects his dots, readers are plunged into alternative universes which forever alter their view of "reality." His books include: *"Happy Trails To High Weirdness," "The Who's Who Of The Manson Family,"* and *"Caught In The Crossfire."* He lives in Southern California – where else?
www.adamgorightly.com

NICK REDFERN

Nick Redfern is a full-time author and journalist specializing in a wide range of unsolved mysteries, including Bigfoot, the Loch Ness Monster, UFO sightings, government conspiracies, alien abductions and paranormal phenomena. His bestselling books include: *"Bloodline of the Gods: Unravel the Mystery in the Human Blood Type to Reveal the Aliens Among Us," "Weapons of the Gods: How Ancient Civilizations Almost Destroyed the Earth,"* and *"The Real Men In Black: Evidence, Famous Cases, and True Stories of These Mysterious Men and their Connection to UFO Phenomena."*
http://nickredfernfortean.blogspot.com/

PROJECT ALIEN MIND CONTROL -- UFO REVIEW SPECIAL

Would You Like Our FREE Catalog? Write or send an email and let us know!

Global Communications, PO Box 753, New Brunswick, NJ 08903

Mrufo8@hotmail.com